Edward Arber, Richard Barnfield

Poems

1594-1598

Edward Arber, Richard Barnfield

Poems
1594-1598

ISBN/EAN: 9783744705400

Printed in Europe, USA, Canada, Australia, Japan

Cover: Foto ©Thomas Meinert / pixelio.de

More available books at **www.hansebooks.com**

𝕮𝖍𝖊 𝕰𝖓𝖌𝖑𝖎𝖘𝖍 𝕾𝖈𝖍𝖔𝖑𝖆𝖗'𝖘 𝕷𝖎𝖇𝖗𝖆𝖗𝖞.

RICHARD BARNFIELD,
of Darlaston, Staffordshire, Esquire.

Poems.

1594–1598.

Edited by EDWARD ARBER,
HON. FELLOW OF KING'S COLLEGE, LONDON; F.S.A.,
PROFESSOR OF ENGLISH LANGUAGE AND LITERATURE,
SIR JOSIAH MASON'S COLLEGE, BIRMINGHAM.

1, MONTAGUE ROAD, BIRMINGHAM.
15 August, 1882.
No. 14.
(*All rights reserved.*)

CONTENTS.

	PAGE
Bibliography	vii
First Lines of Poems and Stanzas	viii–x
INTRODUCTION	xi–xxiv

The Affectionate Shepheard. Containing the Complaint of Daphnis for the loue of Ganymede   1

    ["Nothing else, but an imitation of *Virgill*, in the second Egologue of *Alexis*," *p.* 44.]

Daphnis [BARNFIELD] Verse-Dedication to Lady Penelope Rich (Sir PHILIP SIDNEY's *STELLA*)   3
The Teares of an affectionate Shepheard sicke for Loue. Or The Complaint of *Daphnis* for the Loue of *Ganimede*   5–24
The Second Dayes Lamentation of the *Affectionate Shepheard*   12–24
The Shepherds Content or the happines of a harmless life ...   25–33
Sonnet   34
The Complaint of Chastitie, &c.   35–37
Hellens Rape, or a light Lanthorne for light Ladies. Written in English Hexameters   38–40

Cynthia. With certaine Sonnets, and the Legend of Cassandra 41–80

Dedication to the Earle of Darby   43
To the curteous Gentlemen Readers   44
T. T. in commendation of the *Authour his worke*   45
[R. BARNFIELD] To his Mistresse   46
Cynthia 47–52
[Sonnets] 53–63
An Ode 64–66
Cassandra 67–80

	PAGE
The Encomion of Lady Pecunia: or The praise of Money	81–93
To the Gentlemen Readers	83–84
The prayse of Lady Pecunia	85–93
His Prayer to Pecunia	93
The Complaint of Poetrie, for the Death of Liberalitie	95–105
Verse-Dedication to Master *Edward Leigh*, of Grayes Inne	97
The Complaint of Poetrie, for the Death of Liberalitie	98–105
The Combat, betweene Conscience and Couetousnesse, in the minde of Man	107–114
Verse-Dedication to Maister *Iohn Steuenton*, of *Dothill*, in the County of *Salop*, Esquire	109
The Combat betweene Conscience and Couetousnesse in the mind of Man	110–114
Poems: in diuers humours	115–124
Verse-Dedication to Master *Nicholas Blackleech*, of Grayes Inne	117
Sonnet I. To his friend Maister R. L. *In praise of Musique and Poetrie*	118
Sonnet II. *Against the Dispraysers of Poetrie*	119
A Remembrance of some English Poets	119–120
An Ode	120–121
Written, at the Request of a Gentleman, vnder a Gentlewoman's Picture	122
An Epitaph vpon the Death, of Sir *Philip Sidney*, Knight	122
An Epitapth vpon the Death of his Aunt, Mistresse *Elizabeth Skrymsher*	123
A Comparison of the Life of Man	124

BIBLIOGRAPHY.

A. *The Affectionate Shepheard, &c.*, by itself.

1. [November] 1594. London, 4to. See title at *p.* 1. The month is fixed by the passage on *p.* 44. Not entered at Stationers' Hall. Two copies known; at Sion College and Britwell.

7. 1842. London, 8vo. *Percy Society.* Vol. 20. Edited by J. O. HALLIWELL-PHILLIPPS, Esq., F.R.S.

B. *Cynthia, &c.*, by itself.

2. [January] 1595. London, 8vo. See title at *p.* 41. Entered at Stationers' Hall on 17th January, 1595. *Transcript.* ii. 669. *Ed.* 1875. The only copy is in the Bodleian Library, Malone's books.

6. 1841. Ryde, Isle of Wight, 12mo. *Beldornie Press.* Printed by Mr. E. V. UTTERSON, who states that he had never seen the *Affectionate Shepheard.* An impression of 16 copies only.

C. *The Encomion of Lady Pecunia, &c.*, by itself.

3. 1598. London, 4to. See title at *p.* 81, and sub-titles at *pp.* 95, 107, and 115. Not entered at Stationers' Hall. One copy known.

4. 1605. London, 4to. Newly corrected and enlarged by RICHARD BARNFIELD, Graduate in Oxford. Two copies known. There are variations from the first edition in this text. Dr. GEORGE KINGSLEY has been good enough to verify the fresh *Dedication* of this new edition at *p.* 84, from the Bridgewater House copy.

A manuscript transcript of this edition is in Ashmolean MS. 1153, at Oxford.

5. 1816. Auchinleck, Dumfriesshire, 4to. *Roxburghe Club.* A facsimile impression of 35 copies printed by JAMES SUTHERLAND, for ALEXANDER BOSWELL; and presented by his brother, JAMES BOSWELL, to the Roxburghe Club. B. M. 8104/4. A copy of the *text only* of this reprint is in the British Museum, 1077. e. 11.

8. 1866. [Maidenhead] 4to. *Illustrations of old English Literature,* i. Edited by J. PAYNE COLLIER, Esq., F.S.A. An impression of 50 copies.

D. The three Collections of Poems together.

9. 1876. London, 4to. *Roxburghe Club.* The Complete Poems. Edited with Introduction and Notes, by the Rev. ALEXANDER B. GROSART, LL.D. About 40 copies printed.

This edition also includes a reprint of the Isham MS., which "is a small paper book of eighteen leaves, within a vellum skin," in the possession of Sir CHARLES H. ISHAM, Lamport Hall, Northampton. Some of the lines in this commonplace book may be by BARNFIELD.

Dr. GROSART also gives the poem from *England's Helicon,* which he thinks may also be by BARNFIELD.

See also Dr. GROSART's 50-copy reprint of SAMUEL NICHOLSON's *ACOLASTUS his After-witte,* for possible imitations of BARNFIELD.

10. 15 August, 1882. Birmingham, 8vo. The present impression.

FIRST LINES OF POEMS AND STANZAS.

	PAGE		PAGE		PAGE
A CANDLE light, and	16	And with this sentence	51	But what talke I of	87
Admit thou come, into...	88	And yet the siluer-noted	18	But when the Worlde ...	86
Againe, we read of old...	15	Another while he wooes	30	But who can liue with ...	99
Against my Birth-day ..	14	A paire of Kniues, a......	14	But who can shun the...	75
A guilded Nutmeg, and	14	Apply thy minde to be	21	But yet shee rather......	37
Ah be not stained	17	As for example, in the..	19	By thee great *Collin*...	31
Ah fairest *Ganymede* ...	60	As for the young man ...	87	By this the formost	49
Ah, little knew *Matilda*	36	A Shepheard loues no ...	32	By this, the Night.........	24
Ah no ; nor I my selfe :	62	As it fell vpon a Day ...	120	By this, young *Phœbus*	67
Ah therefore be not	70	Aye mee (distressed	113		
Alas poore *Conscience* ...	112			CHAUCER is dead ; and	119
Alas (the while) that......	7	BE[A]UTY and Maiesty	54	Cherry-lipt *Adonis* in ...	61
All these, and more	10	Behold my grey head....	23	Compare the Cow and...	18
All which he eloquently	69	Be not beguild with	21	Compare the loue of......	11
Also if any proue a	30	Be not offensiue to the...	21	Compare the Wyld-cat...	19
And albeit the gift be ...	3	Be patient in extreame...	23		
And alwaies (I am sure)	11	Betwixt amaze and	72	DEEPE-wounding Arrow	31
And as the Coyne, she...	91	*Bounty* looke backe	102	*Diana* (on a time).........	57
And at the same time ...	6	Bright Starre of Beauty	46	Downe in a Dale, hard	48
And *Bounty*, though her	105	Bugle and Ieat, with ...	19	Downe sliding from that	45
And *Daniell*, praised for	119	But ah (alas) how can ...	46		
And *Drayton*, whose ...	119	But ah (alas) my Teares	104	EUEN as a counterfeited	112
And euery Morne by ...	8	But ah, she cannot (or...	105	Euen as *Apelles* could ...	122
And (for thy sake) this...	72	But as the woefull......	104	Euen as the Sunne	101
And from her Iuory	67	But (*Bounty*) if thou ...	102		
And hauing both their...	6	But faire *Pecunia*.........	89	FAINE would she haue	78
And hearing that her ...	74	But her an Old-Man......	6	Faire-long-haire-wearing	15
And herein happie, I ...	102	But if the first did.........	76	Faire *Penthesilea* th' ...	68
And if he so escape with	28	But if thou wilt not	11	Faire *Philomela*, cease	100
And in the sweltring......	8	But if you want your ...	88	Farre be it from my......	75
And last of all, if any ...	30	But I that lou'd thee for	11	*Fayre louely Ladie* ...	3
And last of all, in blacke	30	But I, whose hope is ...	103	Fie on ambition, fie on	79
And manie thousand ...	10	But leaue we him in.....	7	First he ordaines by Act	29
And meaning now to ...	70	But let mee feele the...	32	First, in a royall Chaire	48
And *Shakespeare*	120	But *Liberalitie* is dead	99	Fond Loue is blinde ...	16
And sith there dies no ...	103	But not preuailing.........	74	Fond Wretch, it was not	113
(And tells her softly in...	69	But now good-fortune...	33	For as by death, her......	80
And thou art shee, O ...	90	But now my Muse.........	63	For her, the Merchant...	88
And though I cannot ...	46	But now to her, whose...	91	For her, the Gentleman	88
And thou loue-hating...	23	But now vnto her	88	For if we doo consider...	19
And thou loue-scorning	12	But she no sooner had...	71	For pledge that I am ...	77
And thou *Melpomene* ...	100	But sleepe his soule in...	29	For when his stately......	15
And thou my sweete......	29	But sure it is not	102	For why against the......	86
And thus it hapned	6	But this braue generall	75		
And to conclude, the ...	51	But to *Cassandra* now	73	GODDESSE of Golde	85
And when he hath her	87	But to returne to these...	75	Great Lady, sith I haue	93
And when it pleaseth ...	8	But what care they	87	Great was the mone ...	73
And when th'art wearie	13	But what? (fond man)	76	HAD I the sweet	92
				Happy are they, that ...	79
				He and *Cassandra* now	77

First Lines of Poems and Stanzas. ix

	PAGE		PAGE		PAGE
Heare Shepheards oft ...	22	Liue *Spenser* euer, in ...	119	Or if thou list to bathe...	9
Hee briefly t'her relates	69	Loe here beholde the ...	123	Or if thou dar'st to	9
Hee intertaines her	86	Loe here behold these ...	34	Or if thou lou'st to heare	9
Hee needes not feare ...	87	Long haue I long'd to ...	61	Or if thoult goe vnto...	9
Heerewith awaking	72	Looke how a brightsome	71	Or if thou wilt goe......	13
He is a Courtier, for he	33	*Louely a Lasse, so*	38	Or in a mystic morning	13
He is not troubled with	25	Lyke to an other	91	Or when bad subiects ...	26
He leads his Wench a...	31			Or with Hare-pypes......	13
He (noble Lord)	77	MANS life is vvell	124	Or wilt thou drinke a...	14
Here ended shee; and..	79	Monster of Art	36	O that my Teares could	105
Here, hold this gloue ...	60	My hand, to helpe mee	103	O that Nobilitie, it selfe	101
Here, on love's altar......	34			O who can comfort my...	98
Here-with, as weary of...	80	NAY more for money ...	92	O who can then	88
Here-with she blushing	70	Nay more than this	10		
He sits all Day	29	Nere-waining...............	45	PRAISE not thy selfe, let	23
Him leaue me (for a......	71	Neuer againe, shall I ...	100	Pride looks aloft, still ...	17
His Iuory-white and ...	5	New Coyne is coynd ...	91		
How happie were a	32	Next Morning when the	12	QUEENE of my thoughts	73
How on the Seas he......	76	Nights were short, and	64		
Humillity in misery is...	17	No Briefes nor	25	RAYS'D from the cynders	45
Humillity is clad in	17	No flocke of sheepe, but	91	Remember Age, and ...	17
		Nor is the Derth of	104	Restrain thy steps from	23
I DEEMED so; nor was I	49	Not faire, *Adonis* in his	68	Right Diamonds are of	19
If chafed on thy haire ...	90	Not faire *Hesione*	91		
If it be sinne to loue a...	5	Not *Megabates* nor	62	SALMON and Trout are...	20
If Musique and sweet ...	118	Not proud *Alcyous* ...	9	Scarce had *Apollo*.........	68
If *Pythias* death, of	103	Not th'hungry Lyon ...	71	Scarce had the morning	5
If thou wilt come and !..	10	Now doth he stroke......	7.	Scarce had the Syren ..	77
If thou wilt loue me......	12	Now had the poore-mans	79	Scarce was the louely ...	74
If wealth? Why	99	Now had the cole-blacke	110	Scarce were these.........	70
I haue a pleasant noted	14	Now is she ioylesse	78	Sell thy sweet breath to	16
I liu'd (quoth she) to see	79	Now nimbly to his	71	Serue *Ioue* (vpon thy ...	21
I loued once, (quoth hee)	69	Now silent night drew...	78	She wakes the lecher ...	77
Image of that, whose ...	97	Now sleepeth shee	72	She, weepes; he, wooes	74
Impartiall *Parcæ*, will...	105	Now was the Welkyn ...	47	Sighing, and sadly	58
I neuer then, did write	98	Now with a trice he......	68	Siluer and Golde, and ...	90
Innumerable be the......	20			Sith Conscience (long ...	109
In *Pan* repose thy trust	22	O *ADULATION*, Canker	101	So *Cytheræa* would	105
Insteede of teares, he ...	76	Obtaine a faithfull frend	22	So darke the dungeon ...	78
In Westerne world amids	51	O fading Branches of ...	28	Some Courtiers carefull	27
In which delight feeding	49	O faire Boy trust not to	18	Some talke of *Ganymede*	59
I promis'd wealth	50	O faire-foule Tincture ...	35	Sometimes I wish that...	57
I sing not of *Angellica*	85	O fairest, faire, aboue ...	68	Speake Eccho, tell	59
I spi'd him first, and ...	50	Of all the kindes of	25	Sporting at fancie	53
It is reported of faire ...	55	O glorious Sunne quoth	12	Sporting our selues to ...	49
I would put amber	8	Oh cruell Fortune.........	78	Sweare no vaine oathes	21
		Oh cruell *Parcæ*	76	Sweet Corrall lips	56
KING *Pryam* dead and	74	Oh foule Eclipser of......	16	Sweet *Thames* I honour	56
		Oh how the *Troyan*......	78	SYDNEY. The Syren	28
LEARNE of the	16	Oh lend thine yuorie ...	16		
Leaue *Guendolen*	9	Oh then be humble	17	TAKE not a flattring......	22
Leaue wicked things ...	21	Oh then be not so proud	20	*Terence* describeth	102
Led by the swift report	84	Oh would I were, as......	105	That *England* lost, that	122
Lie there (quoth shee)...	79	Oh would shee would ...	7	The Courtier he fawn's	26
Lift vp thy head, thou...	76	Oh would to God he......	8	The day shall come	75
Like a great King he ...	29	On th'other side, aboue	48	The greater that I feele	101
		Or if one stray to feede	30	The hardest steele with	24

x First Lines of Poems and Stanzas.

	PAGE		PAGE		PAGE
The iuyce of grapes	93	This is my Doome	37	What fæmale now	36
The Knight, the Squire	27	This leare I learned of...	23	What man, hath lately...	100
The learned Sisters	20	This said *Apollo* then	73	What shall I say to thee	36
The losse of her, is loose	104	This said : he sweetly ...	70	What, ten-yeeres siedge	74
The maimed Souldier ...	104	This was the doting	7	What Thing is then, so	89
The Meane is best, and	85	This was that faire and	7	What though with	31
The Merchants wife	103	Thou dost entice the...	36	When I poore forelorne	24
Thé mightie Monarch ...	26	Thou lazie man	47	VVhen loe, *Cassandra*	72
The more I weepe, the	32	Thou shalt (indeede)	72	When nothing could	89
Then call'd he vp the ...	52	Thou *Venus*, art my	50	When *Saturne* liu'd	86
Then how can I	93	Thou wast the Nurse ...	100	When will my May	11
Then how shall I	92	Thus as they wandred ...	6	Where is *Mecænas*	99
Then shouldst thou	8	Thus doo I honour thee	11	Whether yee list, to	92
Then sith by mee, their	99	Thus doth he frollicke it	31	Which charge to him no	69
Then, sith the Pope is ...	92	Thus doth he keepe	30	Which done : relying on	71
Then Teares (if thou be	34	Thus euerie man is	28	Which saying to be true	75
Then will I lay out all...	14	Thus haue I shew'd the	50	Which with Quick	90
The Painful	28	Thus haue I showed in	33	White is the colour of ...	20
The peoples ioies	77	Thus is he neuer full ...	26	Who would not then a...	33
The Pinke, the	10	Thus, sacred Virgin ...	52	Why doo thy Corall lips	15
The Queene of harts	90	Thus was my loue, thus	58	Whylom that in a	45
There are so manie	33	Thus with the Worlde ...	86	Why should thy sweete	15
The reason is, because...	89	Thy tyme was once ...	90	VVhich when *Aurora* ...	73
Therefore as one, whose	102	To what vse serues a ...	19	Wilt thou set springes in	13
There growes the	10	To you that know the...	117	With her, the Tenant ...	93
There might one see ...	48	Two stars there are in ...	55	With patience, haue I ...	111
These two examples by	15			Witnesse the trade of ...	89
The Skilful Scholler ...	27	VILE *Auarice*, why hast	103	Witnes these watrie eyes	12
The snow is white, and	18	Vile *Auaricia*, how	98	VVit without wealth is...	51
The Stoicks thinke	54	Vpon a gorgious gold ...	67	VVoon with thy words	70
The tenor of which tale	69	Vpon a time the	6		
The Trees (for sorrowe)	100	Vpon a time, the craftie	101	YEA what more	18
The Tyme was once	89	Vpon his head he wore a	68	Yet famous *Sabrine* on	73
The young man	86	Vse not thy louely lips...	22	Yet if thou wilt but	13
The wealthie Merchant	27			Yet not so softly but	67
The whitest siluer is	18	WEEPE Heauens now ...	98	Yet (O Enthraller of...	32
The whylst the other ...	26	Weepe still mine eies ...	101	Yet would I wish, the ...	92
The Wife of *Hector* ...	104	Well is he tearmd a	27	You modest Dames	35
Thinke on thy graue ...	22	What can thy hart	88	You, you alone, can	89

INTRODUCTION.

ONSIDERING the way in which his name has been associated with that of SHAKESPEARE; it is a strange thing that the present should be the first public reprint of BARNFIELD's *Poems* ever made.

During this century, as will be seen from the *Bibliography* at *p.* vii., several limited editions (chiefly of some 16, 35, 40, or 50 copies each) have been produced of one or other of his three Collections of Poems: all the copies of all which impressions would barely number 400; and being for the most part privately printed, they are not now obtainable for either love or money. And, even if they were obtainable, it would be found that some of their texts were intentionally imperfect.

Dr. GROSART's edition of 1876 is notable, among other things, as being the first collected edition put forth, either by BARNFIELD or any one else, of these *Poems*.

II.

HE confused ignorance prevailing respecting BARNFIELD's life before Dr. GROSART's researches recovered the registries of his birth and death with a copy of his Will, may be seen in so recent a Work, as the last edition of T. WARTON's *History of English Poetry*, iv. 290, 436–440. *Ed.* 1871.

It may therefore be desirable to give here, the few undoubted facts that are, at present, known about him.

The Rev. T. BURNE, M.A., Rector of Norbury, near Newport, Shropshire, has most obligingly verified the following entries in the Register of that parish :—

1. Of the marriage of our Poet's parents.

    RICHARDUS BARNEFIELD et MARIA SKRIMSHER matri. contraxere Aprillis xvi. [1572].

2. Of our Poet's birth.

    RICARDUS BARNEFIELD baptizatus fuit die mensis [June] xiii. 1574.

INTRODUCTION.

3. Of the death of his mother, at the birth of his sister DOROTHEA, when our Poet was six years old.

> DOROTHEA BARNEFIELD filia RICARDI BARNEFIELD baptizata fuit Martii xxv. [1581].
> MARIA BARNEFIELD sepulta fuit die mensis p[ræ]d[icto] xxii°

As Dr. GROSART has mentioned, the above names may be read BARNSFIELD.

It is clear from the poem at *p.* 123, that his aunt, ELIZABETH SKRIMSHER, became a second mother to the young boy; and that he ever felt grateful to her.

MALONE contributed the following to BOSWELL's presentation edition of *Lady Pecunia*, of 1816.

> Braze Nose Coll.   November 27, 1589.
> *Richard Barnfield, Stafford, gen. fil. ætat.* 15.
> Matriculated.   *Regtm. Universitat Oxon.*

WOOD took no notice of BARNFIELD. Dr. BLISS (in the life of our Poet supplied by him to his edition of the *Athenæ Oxonienses*, i. 683. Ed. 1813) states that BARNFIELD took his B.A. degree 5 February, 1592; giving as his authority, *MS. Gough*, in Bibl. Bodl. Oxon. I : adding :

"And in the following Lent [1592] performed the exercise for his master's gown; to which, however, I cannot find that he was ever admitted. Certain it is, that he did not take this degree previous to the year 1600, as his name does not occur in the Register of Congregation, which is very perfect and regular about that period."

The exact reference is *Gough's MSS. (Oxfordshire)* I* *p.* 204 : but a better authority for the degree, is WOOD's own transcript (*MS.* F. 14), *sub anno*, where he writes the name RICHARD BARIFIELD.

It has been thought that our Poet when he came to London, entered Gray's Inn : but his name does not occur in the Index of Admittances covering his lifetime, now *Harl. MS.* 1912.

He was evidently the friend of THOMAS WATSON ; of whom he thus writes, at *p.* 29,

> And thou my sweete *Amintas* vertuous minde,
> Should I forget thy Learning or thy Loue ;
> Well might I be accounted but vnkinde,
> Whose pure affection I so oft did proue :
> Might my poore Plaints hard stones to pitty moue ;
>   His losse should be lamented of each Creature,
>   So great his Name, so gentle was his Nature.

In November, 1594, *æt.* 20, appeared *The Affectionate Shepheard.*
In the following January, 1595, *æt.* 21, the *Cynthia* was published.
In 1598, *æt.* 25, he issued *The Encomion of Lady Pecunia,* a quotation

from which is made, in the September of that year, by FRANCIS MERES, in his *Palladis Tamia*; who in the following passage calls him his *friend*.

As *Theocritus* in Greeke, *Virgil* and *Mantuan* in Latine, *Sannazar* in Italian, and [*Thomas Watson*] the Author of *Amintæ Gaudia* and *Walsinghams Melibœus* are the best for Pastoral: so amongst vs the best in this kind are *Sir Philip Sidney*, Master *Challoner*, *Spenser*, *Stephen Gosson*, *Abraham Fraunce*, and *Barnfield*.

As noble *Mæcenas* that sprang from the Etruscan Kings, not only graced poets by his bounty, but also by being a poet himself; and as *James VI.*, now King of *Scotland*, is not only a favourer of poets, but a poet; as my friend Master *Richard Barnfield* hath in this distich passing well recorded,

> *The King of* Scots *now living is a poet,*
> *As his* Lepanto *and his* Furies *show it* [see p. 119].

so *Elizabeth*, our dread Sovereign and gracious Queen. . . .

In 1605, BARNFIELD, *æt.* 31, put forth a new and altered edition of *Lady Pecunia*: and from this time, apparently, ceased to publish anything; probably living the life of a country gentleman in Staffordshire.

In this second Edition of 1605, seven fresh Stanzas, suggested by the new King that had come to the throne, are inserted after the Stanzas which appear on *p.* 91 of this edition: viz., the five following after

No garden can be cleansd of euery Weede.

37

But now more Angels than on Earth yet weare
Her golden Impresse; haue to Heauen attended
Hir Virgin-soule; now, now she soiornes there,
Tasting more ioyes then may be comprehended.
    Life, she hath changde for life (oh countless gaine)
    An earthlie rule, for an eternall Raigne.

38

Such a Successor leauing in her stead,
So peerlesse worthie, and so Royall wise;
In him her vertues liue, though she be dead:
Bountie and zeale, in him both soueranize.
    To him alone, Pecunia doth obay,
    He ruling her, that doth all others sway.

39

Bounty, that when she sickned, cras'd and fainted,
And when she left the earth had almost died;
Hoping with her, in heauen to haue bin sainted,
And 'mongst' the rest an Angels place supplyed:
  The King hath cherisht, and his life assured,
  And of a long consumption, Bounti 's cured.

40

Plenty and Peace vpon his Throne attend,
Health and Content, vpon his person wait:
Conquest and Fame, his Royaltie defend,
May all good Planets smile vpon his state.
  By whom all-drooping-vertues are reuiued,
  And dying-Bounty, made againe long liued.

41

The hand of Heauen still take him to his keeping,
Him, in no danger, in no doubt forsaking;
A thousand of his Angels guarde him sleeping,
And all the hoast of heauen protect him waking.
  That he in safety, peace and rest, may raigne,
  whilst the two Poles, the frame of heuen sustain.

Then another, the sixth, after
But charms the eare, with heauenly Harmonie.

45

Stand forth who can and tell, and true lie saie
When England, Scotland, Ireland and France,
He euer saw Pecunia to displaie
Before these daies; O wondrous happie chance.
  Nor doth Pecunia onelie please the eie,
  But charmes the eare, with heauenlie harmony.

And a seventh after
Yet is it worth but *Nine-pence*, at the most.

47
But Ireland alone, this Musicks sound
Being clad in Siluer, challenge for their coin
What though amongst vs much thereof be found
Authoritie, no subject dooth inioyne
  Aboue his worth to countenance the same,
  Then men, not coin, are worthy of that blame.

BARNFIELD died at the early age of 52, leaving, as his will shews, a son and grandchild.

Thanks to Dr. GROSART, we know the year of his death; of which the following record in the Register of St. Michael's, Stone, has been most kindly compared once more with the original, by the Rev. W. W. BAYLISS, M.A., Vicar of that parish.

Nonima eorum qui sepulti erant Anno Domini 1626.
[*i.e.*, between 25 March, 1626, and 24 March, 1627.]

Then after about thirty entries, we have the following one :

Richardus Barnefield generosus sepultus
fuit Sexto Die Martij Anno supradicto.

Then comes one more entry : after which we have the following official signatures for the year :

BARNABAS WILLATT	Minister.
JAMES TILL	
THOMAS AMBERYE	Churchwardens.
ROGER BRADBURYE	
CHRISTOPHER DUTTON	

We have personally inspected our Poet's Will, in the District Probate Court at Lichfield. It is Number 57, of *anno* 1627, and is, line for line, as follows :

In the name of god Amen the xxvjth Daye februarie in the yeares of the Raigne of our Soveraigne lord CHARLES by the grace of god of England Scotland ffrance and Ireland kinge Defender of the faith &c *Anno Dom.* 1626 [*i.e.*, 1627]. `

I RICHARD BARNFIELD of Dorlestone in the Countie of Stafford Esquire sick in bodie but of perfecte Remembrance make this my last will and testament in manner and fforme ffollowinge/ffirst I bequeath my soule to Almightie god my Creator and maker and my Bodie to be buried in the parishe Church of Stone in the said Countie in full hope of of salvation and of a ioyfull Resurrectione thrught Christ my onelie Saviour, and as concerninge my worldlie goodes my will and mind is that Master JOHN SKRIMSHER of Norburie Esquier his wife and sonne˙ shall haue iij*li* beinge equallie Devided betwixt them, *Item* I giue to Master HENERIE HOCKENGULL my peece, Dagg, one Beddsteed one table, my best sadle and bridle, *Item* I giue to Mistris HOCKENGULL xxs. *Item* I giue to CHARLES SKRIMSHER and GERRATE SKRIMSHER ether of them xxs. *Item* I giue to mistris ELENOR SKRIMSHER xxs. *Item* I giue to SARIE BOEYER xxs. *Item* I giue to ELIZABETH SKRIMSHER xxs. and alsoe one gould Ringe *Item* I giue to MARTHA xxs. and my gilte spoone *Item* I giue to GRIESELL SKRIMSHER xxs. *Item* I giue my gran[d]childe JANE BARNEFEILD a gilte saulte which was MICHILL OFFELEYes if hee Doe not Redeeme the same in some short tyme But if hee Doe Redeeme it shee shall haue the whole xj*li* that he Doth owe me *Item* I giue to master MARTIN xs. *Item* I giue to my man RICHARD COTTERALL xls. my hare coulred sute and Cloake and xs. that I owe him, *Item* I giue to mistris DOODIE my Truckle bedd *Item* I giue to my Cozen RANFORDE my tow best sutes, *Item* I giue MARGARET RICHARSONE my goune and xs. *Item* I giue GEORGE HILL my ould servant my other sadle and Bridle, *Item* I giue to euerie servant in the house xij*d*. *Item* I leaue v*li*. to bestowe of a Dinner at my Buriall *Item* I giue to the poore of Darlestone xij*d* a peece *Item* I give to the poor of Stone xls. *Item* I give to JOHN GOODALE of waulton my blue breeches and friese Jerkine *Item* I giue to my sonne master ROBERT BARNEFIELD xxs. *Item* the Residue of my goodes beinge vnbequeathed, I giue to master ROBERT

INTRODUCTION. xvii

BARNEFIELD and mistris ELINOR SKRIMSHER whome I leaue my sole Executors of this my last will and testament In witness whereof the Daie and yeare aboue written I have putt my hand and seale

Sealed and subscribed in presence of vs

R.
[*Initial only.*]

Henry hockengull
Thomas Daintry

Richard Cotterell

Probate was granted ELEANOR SKRIMSHER, on 7th April, 1627. With the Will is the following Inventory :

John Doodie.
Richard Challenor.
Thomas Daintery.
PETER SERIEANTES
his X mark.

A true and perfecte Inventorie of all the goodes of RICHARD BARNEFEILD esquire Deceased [ap]praysed th xvth Daie of March *AnnoDomini* 1626 [*i.e.* 1627] by JOHN DOODIE RICHARD CHALLENOR THOMAS DAINTREY PETER SERIEANTE/

It[*em*] my tuw beddsteds	vjs	viij*d*
item one flockbedd	iijs	iiij*d*
item one bedd one boulster one pillowe one coverlid one cadware and three blankettes	iij*li*	
item nine sheetes three pillowberes [*pillow slips*] and one Towell	xxjs	
item fo[u]re shirtes	xiijs	iiij*d*
item Caps	iiijs	
item bandes cuffes handcarches and sockes	xs	
item stockens garters and sockes	xs	
item gloues	ijs	vj*d*
item all his w[e]aringe apperell	x*li*	
item tow sadd[l]es and bridles	xs	
item his bookes	xs	
item one giult sault and spoone	v*li*	
item all his glasses	iiijs	

xviii *INTRODUCTION.*

item pewter [*i.e., vessels &c.*]	vijs	
item three chestes one deske boxes and table	xiijs	iiij*d*
item warminge pan and one close stoole	vjs	viij*d*
item fireshovell tonges and grate	js	
item bootes shooes and slipers	xs	
item one locke and fetters	js	
item one peece and pistoll .	xiijs	iiij*d*
item one brush and one cushen	js	vj*d*
item in moneyes	xl[*li*] xvijs	iij*d*
Some lxvjli	**xvs**	**11d**

[or rather £66 5*s.* 11*d.*]

III.

F THE four editions of his three Collections of Poems issued in BARNFIELD's lifetime, only *six* copies in all are now known to exist, viz., of

The Affectionate Shepheard	1594.	Two copies; at Britwell, and in Sion College, London.
Cynthia	1595.	One copy, in the Bodleian Library.
The Encomion of (1st Ed.)	1598.	One copy, in the Bodleian Library.
Lady Pecunia (2nd Ed.)	1605.	Two copies, at Bridgewater House, and the imperfect one in the Bodleian.

It is probably owing to this extraordinary scarcity of the original copies, that BARNFIELD has made so little impression upon posterity (the *Passionate Pilgrim* matter apart); and has been looked upon as one of our most out-of-the-way Poets.

The notices of our Author, in the first two centuries after his death, appear to have been but few and far between.

EDWARD PHILLIPS omitted our Author in his List of *Modern Poets* in his *Theatrum Poetarum* : but in the *Supplement* thereof, says

Richard *Barnfield*, one of the same Rank in Poetry with Doctor *Lodge*, *Robert Green*, *Nicholas Breton*, and other Contemporaries already mention'd in the foregoing Treatise of the Moderns. *p.* 231. *Ed.* 1675.

THOMAS WARTON thought our Poet to be

One of the most prominent of the minor literary luminaries of the age of Elizabeth. But as BARNFIELD's writings have more than an ordinary share of merit, and as his name has been associated, in a manner which could not be but flattering to his memory, with that of SHAKESPEARE, it seemed to be desirable to introduce in the present pages a somewhat more copious account of this author and his works. Such a tribute to the memory of BARNFIELD seemed to be due to one who, of all the minor poets of ELIZABETH's reign, may perhaps be fairly regarded as occupying the first place.

The most remarkable feature about BARNFIELD is, that an author of such undoubted genius should have so little courted publicity. In his earliest production, the *Affectionate Shepheard*, 1594, his name nowhere appears [*but the authorship was avowed in the* Cynthia ; *see p.* 44] ; and all his works were ushered unostentatiously into the world without encomiastic verses by acquaintances or admirers, and with dedications prompted, so far as one can judge, by friendship or affection, rather than by the sense of interest or the desire to flatter.
History of English Poetry, iv. *pp.* 436, 7. *Ed.* 1871.

Then follows the confused account above referred to; after which comes :

A collected edition of BARNFIELD's surviving works is a want in English literature, and would only form an appropriate and deserved tribute to the genius of so graceful and so neglected a poet. *p.* 439. *idem.*

No author, whom we could name, has fairer pretensions to be regarded as a writer of genuine, untainted vernacular English. *p.* 440. *idem.*

IV.

HE association of BARNFIELD's name with that of SHAKESPEARE (which has been the principal reason, hitherto, of his name being kept in remembrance) has arisen from W. JAGGARD's including

the Sonnet *If Musique and sweet Poetrie agree*, at *p.* 118,
and the Ode *As it fell upon a Day*, at *p.* 120.

in *The passionate Pilgrim*, 1599; and from his placing on the title-page of that Collection, the words, *By W. SHAKESPEARE.* The Staffordshire poet being 25, and the Warwickshire poet 35 in that year.

Mr. J. P. COLLIER, F.S.A., has advocated first the BARNFIELD authorship of these poems, and then that of SHAKESPEARE. His several arguments on both sides, are duly recorded by Dr. GROSART, in his edition of our Poet above referred to.

The opinion of the best scholars is generally for the BARNFIELD authorship ; whose claims Mr. CHARLES EDMONDS has especially vindicated at length from the objections of Mr. COLLIER in the *Preface* to his reprint of the Isham copy of *The Passionate Pilgrim*, in 1870.

It may, however, be as well, on the occasion of this reimpression, briefly to summarize the proofs of BARNFIELD being the author of these poems : observing that the claim is, in either case, for *both* poems together, and not for either of them.

1. That BARNFIELD was not the man to steal any one else's poems is evident from the following modest disclaimer, at *p.* 44, of works which had wrongly been attributed to him.

> Howsoeuer undeseruedly (I protest) I haue beene thought (of some) to haue beene the authour of two Books heretofore. I neede not to name them, because they are two-well knowne already: nor will I deny them, because they are dislik't ; but because they are not mine. This protestation (I hope) will satisfie th'indifferent.

The two Works referred to have been thought to be, R. B. Gent. *Greenes Funeralls*, 1594 ; and R. B. Gent. *ORPHEUS his Journey to Hell*, 1595 : but the latter of these, is out of the question ; for it was not registered at Stationers' Hall till the 26 August, 1595 (*Transcript &c.*, iii. 48. *Ed.* 1876) more than six months after the *Cynthia* containing the above passage, was entered for publication.

2. BARNFIELD, on the other hand, thus distinctly claims these pieces with the others, in *Poems in diuers humours*, at *p.* 117.

> I vvrite these Lines ; fruits of vnriper yeares.

3. It is incredible that SHAKESPEARE should have written of any poet in these terms, as in the Sonnet *If Music, &c.*, at *p.* 118,

> *Spenser* to mee ; whose deepe Conceit is such,
> As passing all Conceit, needs no defence.

4. Which lines are evidently BARNFIELD's, for he thus repeats the expression in *A Remembrance of some English Poets* (including SHAKESPEARE himself), on the opposite page : which *Remembrance* has never been attributed to any one else but him.

> Liue *Spenser* euer, in thy *Fairy Queene* :
> Whose like (for deepe Conceit) was neuer seene ;

expressions which perfectly accord with the poetical position of BARNFIELD, who was one of the first professed imitators of SPENSER, *p.* 44.

5. *If Musique, &c.*, is the first of two Sonnets : for the authorship of the Second of which, we have the express testimony of his friend MERES, that it was written by BARNFIELD : see the lines quoted at *p.* xiii. As BARNFIELD was evidently incapable of *stealing* the First sonnet ; this proof that he wrote the latter is corroborative of his having written the former.

6. If BARNFIELD wrote the Sonnet, he wrote also the Ode : for the

poems, in this connection, are inseparable. They were either both written by him, or by SHAKESPEARE. Clearly to BARNFIELD, must the authorship be assigned.

7. But, then, Why did BARNFIELD omit these poems in his second edition of *Lady Pecunia* in 1605? This of course was a somewhat difficult matter to settle without seeing the original edition: and as the only copy known until recently was at Bridgewater House, this was not an easy matter, until the Rev. W. E. BUCKLEY identified the other copy in the Bodleian.

As Mr. COLLIER bases the SHAKESPEARE authorship of these poems *solely* on their omission from the 1605 edition: it is but right to state his later opinion precisely.

" My mistaken notion, twelve years ago [1846] was, that BARNFIELD, in 1605, had republished the whole of what had first appeared in 1598. This is not so. In 1605 he prefixed a general title-page, mentioning only three of the four divisions of his original work. 1. *Lady Pecunia, or The Praise of Money.* 2. *A Combat betwixt Conscience and Covetousness;* and 3. *The Complaint of Poetry, for the Death of Liberality.* He says not one word about what had been his fourth division in 1598, *Poems in divers humours*: but still, on the very last leaf of the impression of 1605, Barnfield places *A Remembrance of some English Poets,* which had appeared as one of the *Poems in divers humours* in 1598. *A Comparison of the Life of Man,* a seven-line stanza, is also reprinted; all the rest he seems purposely to have excluded as if they were not his." *Notes and Queries,* 1856.

" The second edition of BARNFIELD's *Encomion,* under the title of *Lady Pecunia, or The praise of Money,* was not known at all until a comparatively recent date, and still more recently [? *in 1856 as above*] it was discovered that it did not contain the poems to which BARNFIELD seemed to have the earliest title. In 1605 BARNFIELD was too honest to retain what had been improperly attributed to him [*he himself claims them, see above*] in 1598. The Sonnet and the Poem are therefore not to be traced in the volume in our hands, which forms part of the library of Bridgewater house." *Bibliographical and Critical Account of the Rarest Books in the English Language,* i. *pp.* 47-50, *Ed.* 1865.

It will therefore be seen that the assertion of the SHAKESPEARE authorship rests, and rests only on the "make up" of the 1605 edition: without any regard to intrinsic merits, or to any assertion of authorship (as above at 2) on the part of BARNFIELD.

An examination, side by side, of the copies of the two editions in the Malone Collection (Nos. 295 and 300) in the Bodleian, will shew any one practically acquainted with printing, that Mr. COLLIER's references are nothing but random guesses.

The 1605 edition was never intended to be a careful reprint of the 1598 edition, the framework of which, in four distinct sections, was intentionally abandoned.

    a. The Section Title-pages of the First edition (as at *pp.* 95, 107, 115) were discarded.

    b. The Verse-Dedications of the First edition (as at *pp.* 97, 109, 117) were also discarded.

    c. The Sections do not follow in the same order as in the First edition: the *Combat* (*pp.* 107–114) in the second edition precedes the *Complaint* (*pp.* 95–105).

    d. That any of the *Poems in divers humours* were reprinted at all, is clearly owing to this last fact. For the 45th and last stanza of the *Complaint* ends on the top of the page preceding the last leaf. *A Comparison of the Life of Man* (see *p.* 124), therefore, just filled up that page nicely.

    A Remembrance of some English Poets did the same for the opposite page of the last leaf; the final page being left blank.

Therefore no question of authorship arises from the omissions which were purely a publisher's convenience, probably dictated by the price of the book.

It will also be seen that the section *Poems in divers humours* contains eight poems, of which two only were reprinted by BARNFIELD in 1605, "All the rest he seems purposely to have excluded as if they were not his," says Mr. COLLIER: but unfortunately one of these is *An Epitaph upon the Death of his Aunt Mistresse Elizabeth Skrymsher*, whom we know was BARNFIELD's mother's sister.

It is therefore evident that BARNFIELD, and not SHAKESPEARE wrote these poems: and if so, that they should be omitted from all future editions of the *Works* of our great Dramatist.

V.

DISCARDING this modern and unnecessary entanglement, let us see what our Poet really is in himself, remarking that all his Verse is the production of a very young man.

Receiving the usual education given to an English gentleman at the time, this young barrister (as we should now call him), following the fashion of the Age, addicted himself to versification. Between the ages of twenty and twenty-four, he published, in his three Collections, some forty-five pieces, short and long, in different metres, and in varying styles, of what, in the present day, would be looked upon as *vers de société*: that is, skilful poetry, *not* expressing any personal feelings or describing any great epic action or passion.

So that we should not, by any means, consider him, with WARTON, as the first of the minor Elizabethan poets : indeed he seems to us hardly a third-rate poet ; if DRAYTON, DANIEL, CHAPMAN, CAMPION, and such others constituted, then, the second rank of our hierarchy of Makers.

Among other characteristics of these poems, the following are apparent.

1. An abundant vocabulary. Proportionately to their length, there is a large number of different words, and some of them out-of-the-way ones, in these poems.

2. There is evident also, a constant strain after novelty ; either through unusual subjects, or by unusual treatment of ordinary subjects. BARNFIELD avows this, at *p.* 83, in regard to *Lady Pecunia,*

> Being determined to write of something, and yet not resolued of any thing, I considered with my selfe, if one should write of Loue (they will say) why, euery one writes of Loue: if of Vertue, why, who regards Vertue? To be short, I could thinke of nothing, but either it was common, or not at all in request ;

and it is also characteristic of many of his poems.

This craving after something cleverly strange, has laid him open to the charge of equivocal writing ; which disappears at once, when we consider his versification was for the most part but an amusement, and had little serious or personal in it.

He being about twenty years of age, wrote in imitation of VIRGIL his *Affectionate Shepheard,* and the twenty *Sonnets* in *Cynthia* (*pp.* 53–63), to a youth, whom he named GANYMEDE, in the character of an old man thus described at *p.* 23 :

> Behold my gray head, full of siluer haires,
> My wrinckled skin, deepe furrowes in my face :
> Cares bring Old-Age, Old-Age increaseth cares ;
> My Time is come, and I haue run my Race :
>   Winter hath snow'd vpon my hoarie head,
>   And with my Winter all my ioys are dead.

It is clearly a piece of artificiality, a trying after the uncommon.

So likewise, he selected his punning and bantering *Prayse of Lady Pecunia,* because it was unhackneyed.

> At length I bethought my selfe of a Subiect, both new (as hauing neuer beene written vpon before) and pleasing (as I thought) because Mans Nature (commonly) loues to heare that praised, with whose pressence, hee is most pleased. *p.* 83.

3. Another noticeable point is his hearty recognition in verse of the greater merits of recent or contemporary English poets : as of SIDNEY, at *pp.* 28, 31, 119, 122 ; WATSON, at *pp.* 29, 31 ; SPENSER, at *pp.* 31, 118, 119 ; DRAYTON, at *pp.* 31, 119 ; DANIEL, at *p.* 119 ; SHAKESPEARE at *p.* 120 ; with others of an earlier date.

VI.

THE other principal references may be given.

They are, RITSON, *Bibliographia Poetica*, 124, *Ed.* 1802. ELLIS, *Specimens of the English Poets*, ii. 356, *Ed.* 1803. BELOE, *Anecdotes of Literature*, ii. 68, *Ed.* 1807. BODENHAM's *England's Helicon*, 126, *Ed.* 1812. Sir E. BRYDGES, *Restituta*, iv. 490, *Ed.* 1816. *Gentleman's Magazine*, 3 S. xvi. *f.* 159. *Collectanea Anglo-Poetica*, i. 184-6, Cheetham Society, 1860. *Bibliotheca Heberiana*, iv. 15.

VII.

IN CONCLUSION, we cannot refrain from the expression of our gratification at yet another lost English Author being restored to life again, through our instrumentality. How many more are there? We cannot say. Though we have been constantly printing for now nearly fourteen years: there seems more ahead, than behind. Will this Generation own the Endeavour, or shall it be left to Posterity to do so?

The Affectionate
Shepheard.

Containing the Complaint of *Daphnis* for
the loue of *Ganymede*.

Amor plus mellis, quam fellis, est.

LONDON,

Printed by Iohn Danter for T. G. and E. N.
and are to bee sold in Saint Dunstones
Church-yeard in Fleetstreet,
1594.

To the Right Excellent
and most beautifull Lady, the Ladie
PENELOPE RITCH.

Ayre louely Ladie, vvhose Angelique eyes
Are Vestall Candles of sweet Beauties Treasure,
Whose speech is able to inchaunt the wise,
Conuerting Ioy to Paine, and Paine to Pleasure;
  Accept this simple Toy of my Soules Dutie,
  Which I present vnto thy matchles Beautie.

And albeit the gift be all too meane,
Too meane an Offring for thine Iuorie Shrine;
Yet must thy Beautie my iust blame susteane,
Since it is mortall, but thy selfe diuine.
  Then (Noble Ladie) take in gentle vvorth,
  This new-borne Babe which here my Muse brings forth.

Your Honours most affectionate
    and perpetually deuoted Shepheard:
        DAPHNIS.

The Teares of an
affectionate Shepheard sicke for Loue.
OR
The Complaint of *Daphnis* for the Loue of *Ganimede*.

Scarce had the morning Starre hid from the light
Heauens crimson Canopie with stars be-[spangled,
But I began to rue th'vnhappy sight
Of that faire Boy that had my hart in-tangled;
  Cursing the Time, the Place, the sense, the sin;
  I came, I saw, I viewd, I slipped in.

If it be sinne to loue a sweet-fac'd Boy,
(Whose amber locks trust vp in golden tramels
Dangle adowne his louely cheekes with ioy,
When pearle and flowers his faire haire enamels)
  If it be sinne to loue a louely Lad;
  Oh then sinne I, for whom my soule is sad.

His Iuory-white and Alabaster skin
Is staind throughout with rare Vermillion red,
Whose twinckling starrie lights do neuer blin
To shine on louely *Venus* (Beauties bed :)
  But as the Lillie and the blushing Rose,
  So white and red on him in order growes.

Vpon a time the Nymphs bestird them-selues
To trie who could his beautie soonest win:
But he accounted them but all as Elues,
Except it were the faire Queene *Guendolen*,
   Her he embrac'd, of her was beloued,
   With plaints he proued, and with teares he moued.

But her an Old-Man had beene sutor too,
That in his age began to doate againe;
Her would he often pray, and often woo,
When through old-age enfeebled was his Braine :
   But she before had lou'd a lustie youth
   That now was dead, the cause of all her ruth.

And thus it hapned, Death and *Cupid* met
Vpon a time at swilling *Bacchus* house,
Where daintie cates vpon the Board were set,
And Goblets full of wine to drinke carouse :
   Where Loue and Death did loue the licor so,
   That out they fall and to the fray they goe.

And hauing both their Quiuers at their backe
Fild full of Arrows; Th'one of fatall steele,
The other all of gold; Deaths shaft was black,
But Loues was yellow : Fortune turnd her wheele ;
   And from Deaths Quiuer fell a fatall shaft,
   That vnder *Cupid* by the winde was waft.

And at the same time by ill hap there fell
Another Arrow out of *Cupids* Quiuer;
The which was carried by the winde at will,
And vnder Death the amorous shaft did shiuer :
   They being parted, Loue tooke vp Deaths dart,
   And Death tooke vp Loues Arrow (for his part.)

Thus as they wandred both about the world,
At last Death met with one of feeble age:
Wherewith he drew a shaft and at him hurld
The vnknowne Arrow; (with a furious rage)
   Thinking to strike him dead with Deaths blacke dart,
   But he (alas) with Loue did wound his hart.

This was the doting foole, this was the man
That lou'd faire *Guendolena* Queene of Beautie;
Shee cannot shake him off, doo what she can,
For he hath vowd to her his soules last duety:
    Making him trim vpon the holy-daies;
    And crownes his Loue with Garlands made of Baies.

Now doth he stroke his Beard; and now (againe)
He wipes the driuel from his filthy chin;
Now offers he a kisse; but high Disdaine
Will not permit her hart to pity him:
    Her hart more hard than Adamant or steele,
    Her hart more changeable than Fortunes wheele.

But leaue we him in loue (vp to the eares)
And tell how Loue behau'd himselfe abroad;
Who seeing one that mourned still in teares
(a young-man groaning vnder Loues great Load)
    Thinking to ease his Burden, rid his paines:
    For men haue griefe as long as life remaines.

Alas (the while) that vnawares he drue
The fatall shaft that Death had dropt before;
By which deceit great harme did then issue,
Stayning his face with blood and filthy goare.
    His face, that was to *Guendolen* more deere
    Than loue of Lords, of any lordly Peere.

This was that faire and beautifull young-man,
Whom *Guendolena* so lamented for;
This is that Loue whom she doth curse and ban,
Because she doth that dismall chaunce abhor:
    And if it were not for his Mothers sake,
    Euen *Ganimede* himselfe she would forsake.

Oh would shee would forsake my *Ganimede*,
Whose sugred loue is full of sweete delight,
Vpon whose fore-head you may plainely reade
Loues Pleasure, grau'd in yuorie Tables bright:
    In whose faire eye-balls you may clearely see
    Base Loue still staind with foule indignitie.

Oh would to God he would but pitty mee,
That loue him more than any mortall wight;
Then he and I with loue would soone agree,
That now cannot abide his Sutors sight.
   O would to God (so I might haue my fee)
   My lips were honey, and thy mouth a Bee.

Then shouldst thou sucke my sweete and my faire flower
That now is ripe, and full of honey-berries:
Then would I leade thee to my pleasant Bower
Fild full of Grapes, of Mulberries, and Cherries;
   Then shouldst thou be my Waspe or else my Bee,
   I would thy hiue, and thou my honey bee.

I would put amber Bracelets on thy wrests,
Crownets of Pearle about thy naked Armes:
And when thou sitst at swilling *Bacchus* feasts
My lips with charmes should saue thee from all harmes:
   And when in sleepe thou tookst thy chiefest Pleasure,
   Mine eyes should gaze vpon thine eye-lids Treasure.

And euery Morne by dawning of the day,
When *Phœbus* riseth with a blushing face,
Siluanus Chappel-Clarkes shall chaunt a Lay,
And play thee hunts-vp in thy resting place:
   My Coote thy Chamber, my bosome thy Bed;
   Shall be appointed for thy sleepy head.

And when it pleaseth thee to walke abroad,
(Abroad into the fields to take fresh ayre:)
The Meades with *Floras* treasure should be strowde,
(The mantled meaddowes, and the fields so fayre.)
   And by a siluer Well (with golden sands)
   Ile sit me downe, and wash thine yuory hands.

And in the sweltring heate of summer time,
I would make Cabinets for thee (my Loue:)
Sweet-smelling Arbours made of Eglantine
Should be thy shrine, and I would be thy Doue.
   Coole Cabinets of fresh greene Laurell boughs
   Should shadow vs, ore-set with thicke-set Eughes.

Or if thou list to bathe thy naked limbs,
Within the Christall of a Pearle-bright brooke,
Paued with dainty pibbles to the brims;
Or cleare, wherein thyselfe thy selfe mayst looke;
   Weele goe to *Ladon*, whose still trickling noyse,
   Will lull thee fast asleepe amids thy ioyes.

Or if thoult goe vnto the Riuer side,
To angle for the sweet fresh-water fish:
Arm'd with thy implements that will abide
(Thy rod, hooke, line) to take a dainty dish;
   Thy rods shall be of cane, thy lines of silke,
   Thy hooks of siluer, and thy bayts of milke.

Or if thou lou'st to heare sweet Melodie,
Or pipe a Round vpon an Oaten Reede,
Or make thy selfe glad with some myrthfull glee,
Or play them Musicke whilst thy flocke doth feede;
   To *Pans* owne Pipe Ile helpe my louely Lad,
   (*Pans* golden Pype) which he of *Syrinx* had.

Or if thou dar'st to climbe the highest Trees
For Apples, Cherries, Medlars, Peares, or Plumbs,
Nuts, Walnuts, Filbeards, Chest-nuts, Ceruices,
The hoary Peach, when snowy winter comes;
   I haue fine Orchards full of mellowed frute;
   Which I will giue thee to obtain my sute.

Not proud *Alcynous* himselfe can vaunt,
Of goodlier Orchards or of brauer Trees
Than I haue planted; yet thou wilt not graunt
My simple sute; but like the honey Bees
   Thou suckst the flowre till all the sweet be gone;
   And lou'st mee for my Coyne till I haue none.

Leaue *Guendolen* (sweet hart) though she be faire
Yet is she light; not light in vertue shining:
But light in her behauiour, to impaire
Her honour in her Chastities declining;
   Trust not her teares, for they can watonnize,
   When teares in pearle are trickling from her eyes.

If thou wilt come and dwell with me at home;
My sheep-cote shall be strowd with new greene rushes:
Weele haunt the trembling Prickets as they rome
About the fields, along the hauthorne bushes;
   I haue a pie-bald Curre to hunt the Hare:
   So we will liue with daintie forrest fare.

Nay more than this, I haue a Garden-plot,
Wherein there wants nor hearbs, nor roots, nor flowers;
(Flowers to smell, roots to eate, hearbs for the pot,)
And dainty Shelters when the Welkin lowers:
   Sweet-smelling Beds of Lillies and of Roses,
   Which Rosemary banks and Lauender incloses.

There growes the Gilliflowre, the Mynt, the Dayzie
(Both red and white,) the blew-veynd-Violet:
The purple Hyacinth, the Spyke to please thee,
The scarlet dyde Carnation bleeding yet;
   The Sage, the Sauery, and sweet Margerum,
   Isop, Tyme, and Eye-bright, good for the blinde and dumbe.

The Pinke, the Primrose, Cowslip, and Daffadilly,
The Hare-bell blue, the crimson Cullumbine,
Sage, Lettis, Parsley, and the milke-white Lilly,
The Rose, and speckled flowre cald Sops in wine,
   Fine pretie King-cups, and the yellow Bootes,
   That growes by Riuers, and by shallow Brookes.

And manie thousand moe (I cannot name)
Of hearbs and flowers that in gardens grow,
I haue for thee; and Coneyes that be tame,
Yong Rabbets, white as Swan, and blacke as Crow,
   Some speckled here and there with daintie spots:
   And more I haue two mylch and milke-white Goates.

All these, and more, Ile giue thee for thy loue;
If these, and more, may tyce thy loue away:
I haue a Pidgeon-house, in it a Doue,
Which I loue more than mortall tongue can say:
   And last of all, Ile giue thee a little Lambe
   To play withall, new weaned from her Dam.

But if thou wilt not pittie my Complaint,
My Teares, nor Vowes, nor Oathes, made to thy Beautie:
What shall I doo ? But languish, die, or faint,
Since thou dost scorne my Teares, and my Soules Duetie:
   And Teares contemned, Vowes and Oaths must faile;
   For where Teares cannot, nothing can preuaile.

Compare the loue of faire Queene *Guendolin*
With mine, and thou shalt [s]ee how she doth loue thee:
I loue thee for thy qualities diuine,
But She doth loue another Swaine aboue thee:
   I loue thee for thy gifts, She for hir pleasure;
   I for thy Vertue, She for Beauties treasure.

And alwaies (I am sure) it cannot last,
But sometime Nature will denie those dimples:
In steed of Beautie (when thy Blossom's past)
Thy face will be deformed, full of wrinckles:
   Then She that lou'd thee for thy Beauties sake,
   When Age drawes on, thy loue will soone forsake.

But I that lou'd thee for thy gifts diuine,
In the December of thy Beauties waning,
Will still admire (with ioy) those louely eine,
That now behold me with their beauties baning:
   Though Ianuarie will neuer come againe,
   Yet Aprill yeres will come in showers of raine.

When will my May come, that I may embrace thee?
When will the hower be of my soules ioying?
Why dost thou seeke in mirthe still to disgrace mee?
Whose mirth's my health, whose griefe's my harts annoying.
   Thy bane my bale, thy blisse my blessednes,
   Thy ill my hell, thy weale my welfare is.

Thus doo I honour thee that loue thee so,
And loue thee so, that so doo honour thee,
Much more than anie mortall man doth know,
Or can discerne by Loue or Iealozie:
   But if that thou disdainst my louing euer;
   Oh happie I, if I had loued neuer. *Finis.*

        Plus fellis quam mellis Amor.

The second Dayes Lamentation of
the *Affectionate Shepheard.*

Ext Morning when the golden Sunne was risen,
And new had bid good morrow to the Mountaines;
When Night her siluer light had lockt in prison,
Which gaue a glimmering on the christall Fountaines:
   Then ended sleepe: and then my cares began,
   Eu'n with the vprising of the siluer Swan.

O glorious Sunne quoth I, (viewing the Sunne)
That lightenst euerie thing but me alone:
Why is my Summer season almost done?
My Spring-time past, and Ages Autumne gone?
   My Haruest's come, and yet I reapt no corne:
   My loue is great, and yet I am forlorne.

Witnes these watrie eyes my sad lament
(Receauing cisternes of my ceaseles teares),
Witnes my bleeding hart my soules intent,
Witnes the weight distressed *Daphnis* beares:
   Sweet Loue, come ease me of thy burthens paine;
   Or els I die, or else my hart is slaine.

And thou loue-scorning Boy, cruell, vnkinde;
Oh let me once againe intreat some pittie:
May be thou wilt relent thy marble minde,
And lend thine eares vnto my dolefull Dittie:
   Oh pittie him, that pittie craues so sweetly;
   Or else thou shalt be neuer named meekly.

If thou wilt loue me, thou shalt be my Boy,
My sweet Delight, the Comfort of my minde,
My Loue, my Doue, my Sollace, and my Ioy:
But if I can no grace nor mercie finde,
   Ile goe to *Caucasus* to ease my smart,
   And let a Vulture gnaw vpon my hart.

Yet if thou wilt but show me one kinde looke
(A small reward for my so great affection)
Ile graue thy name in Beauties golden Booke,
And shrowd thee vnder *Hellicons* protection;
   Making the Muses chaunt thy louely prayse:
   (For they delight in Shepheards lowly layes.)

And when th'art wearie of thy keeping Sheepe
Vpon a louely Downe, (to please thy minde)
Ile giue thee fine ruffe-footed Doues to keepe,
And pretie Pidgeons of another kinde:
   A Robbin-red-brest shall thy Minstrell bee,
   Chirping thee sweet, and pleasant Melodie.

Or if thou wilt goe shoote at little Birds
With bow and boult (the Thrustle-cocke and Sparrow)
Such as our Countrey hedges can afford's;
I haue a fine bowe, and an yuorie arrow:
   And if thou misse, yet meate thou shalt [not] lacke,
   Ile hang a bag and bottle at thy backe.

Wilt thou set springes in a frostie Night,
To catch the long-billd Woodcocke and the Snype?
(By the bright glimmering of the Starrie light)
The Partridge, Phæsant, or the greedie Grype?
   Ile lend thee lyme-twigs, and fine sparrow calls,
   Wherewith the Fowler silly Birds inthralls.

Or in a mystie morning if thou wilt
Make pit-falls for the Larke and Pheldifare;
Thy prop and sweake shall be both ouer-guilt;
With *Cyparissus* selfe thou shalt compare
   For gins and wyles, the Oozels to beguile;
   Whilst thou vnder a bush shalt sit and smile.

Or with Hare-pypes (set in a muset hole)
Wilt thou deceaue the deep-earth-deluing Coney?
Or wilt thou in a yellow Boxen bole,
Taste with a woodden splent the sweet lythe honey?
   Clusters of crimson Grapes Ile pull thee downe;
   And with Vine-leaues make thee a louely Crowne.

Or wilt thou drinke a cup of new-made Wine
Froathing at top, mixt with a dish of Creame;
And Straw-berries, or Bil-berries in their prime,
Bath'd in a melting Sugar-Candie streame:
   Bunnell and Perry I haue for thee (alone)
   When Vynes are dead, and all the Grapes are gone.

I haue a pleasant noted Nightingale,
(That sings as sweetly as the siluer Swan)
Kept in a Cage of bone; as white as Whale,
Which I with singing of *Philemon* wan:
   Her shalt thou haue, and all I haue beside;
   If thou wilt be my Boy, or else my Bride.

Then will I lay out all my Lardarie
(Of Cheese, of Cracknells, Curds and Clowted-creame)
Before thy male-content ill-pleasing eye:
But why doo I of such great follies dreame?
   Alas, he will not see my simple Coate;
   For all my speckled Lambe, nor milk-white Goate.

Against my Birth-day thou shalt be my guest:
Weele haue Greene-cheeses and fine Silly-bubs;
And thou shalt be the chiefe of all my feast.
And I will giue thee two fine pretie Cubs,
   With two young Whelps, to make thee sport withall,
   A golden Racket, and a Tennis-ball.

A guilded Nutmeg, and a race of Ginger,
A silken Girdle, and a drawn-worke Band,
Cuffs for thy wrists, a gold Ring for thy finger,
And sweet Rose-water for thy Lilly-white hand,
   A Purse of silke, bespangd with spots of gold,
   As braue a one as ere thou didst behold.

A paire of Kniues, a greene Hat and a Feather,
New Gloues to put vpon thy milk-white hand
Ile giue thee, for to keep thee from the weather;
With Phœnix feathers shall thy Face be fand,
   Cooling those Cheekes, that being cool'd wexe red,
   Like Lillyes in a bed of Roses shed.

Why doo thy Corall lips disdaine to kisse,
And sucke that Sweete, which manie haue desired?
That Baulme my Bane, that meanes would mend my misse:
Oh let me then with thy sweete Lips b'inspired;
  When thy Lips touch my Lips, my Lips will turne
  To Corall too, and being cold yce will burne.

Why should thy sweete Loue-locke hang dangling downe,
Kissing thy girdle-steed with falling pride?
Although thy Skin be white, thy haire is browne:
Oh let not then thy haire thy beautie hide;
  Cut off thy Locke, and sell it for gold wier:
  (The purest gold is tryde in hottest fier).

Faire-long-haire-wearing *Absolon* was kild,
Because he wore it in a brauerie:
So that whiche gracde his Beautie, Beautie spild,
Making him subiect to vile slauerie,
  In being hangd: a death for him too good,
  That sought his owne shame, and his Fathers blood.

Againe, we read of old King *Priamus*,
(The haplesse syre of valiant *Hector* slaine)
That his haire was so long and odious
In youth, that in his age it bred his paine:
  For if his haire had not been halfe so long,
  His life had been, and he had had no wrong.

For when his stately Citie was destroyd
(That Monument of great Antiquitie)
When his poore hart (with griefe and sorrow cloyd)
Fled to his Wife (last hope in miserie;)
  Pyrrhus (more hard than Adamantine rockes)
  Held him and halde him by his aged lockes.

These two examples by the way I show,
To proue th'indecencie of mens long haire:
Though I could tell thee of a thousand moe,
Let these suffice for thee (my louely Faire)
  Whose eye's my starre; whose smiling is my Sunne;
  Whose loue did ende before my ioys begunne.

Fond Loue is blinde, and so art thou (my Deare)
For thou seest not my Loue, and great desart;
Blinde Loue is fond, and so thou dost appeare;
For fond, and blinde, thou greeust my greeuing hart:
  Be thou fond-blinde, blinde-fond, or one, or all;
  Thou art my Loue, and I must be thy thrall.

Oh lend thine yuorie fore-head for Loues Booke,
Thine eyes for candles to behold the same;
That when dim-sighted ones therein shall looke
They may discerne that proud disdainefull Dame;
  Yet claspe that Booke, and shut that Cazement light;
  Lest th'one obscurde, the other shine too bright.

Sell thy sweet breath to th'daintie Musk-ball-makers;
Yet sell it so as thou mayst soone redeeme it:
Let others of thy beauty be pertakers;
Els none but *Daphnis* will so well esteeme it:
  For what is Beauty except it be well knowne?
  And how can it be knowne, except first showne?

Learne of the Gentlewomen of this Age,
That set their Beauties to the open view,
Making Disdaine their Lord, true Loue their Page;
A Custome Zeale doth hate, Desert doth rue:
  Learne to looke red, anon waxe pale and wan,
  Making a mocke of Loue, a scorne of man.

A candle light, and couer'd with a vaile,
Doth no man good, because it giues no light;
So Beauty of her beauty seemes to faile,
When being not seene it cannot shine so bright.
  Then show thy selfe and know thy selfe withall,
  Lest climing high thou catch too great a fall.

Oh foule Eclipser of that fayre sun-shine,
Which is intitled Beauty in the best;
Making that mortall, which is els diuine,
That staines the fayre which Womens steeme not least:
  Get thee to Hell againe (from whence thou art)
  And leaue the Center of a Woman's hart.

Ah be not staind, (sweet Boy) with this vilde spot,
Indulgence Daughter, Mother of mischaunce;
A blemish that doth euery beauty blot;
That makes them loath'd, but neuer doth aduaunce
   Her Clyents, fautors, friends; or them that loue her;
   And hates them most of all, that most reproue her.

Remember Age, and thou canst not be prowd,
For age puls downe the pride of euery man;
In youthfull yeares by Nature tis allowde
To haue selfe-will, doo Nurture what she can;
   Nature and Nurture once together met,
   The Soule and shape in decent order set.

Pride looks aloft, still staring on the starres,
Humility looks lowly on the ground;
Th'one menaceth the Gods with ciuill warres,
The other toyles til he haue Vertue found:
   His thoughts are humble, not aspiring hye;
   But Pride looks haughtily with scornefull eye.

Humillity is clad in modest weedes,
But Pride is braue and glorious to the show;
Humillity his friends with kindnes feedes,
But Pride his friends (in neede) will neuer know:
   Supplying not their wants, but them disdaining;
   Whilst they to pitty neuer neede complayning.

Humillity in misery is relieu'd,
But Pride in neede of no man is regarded;
Pitty and Mercy weepe to see him grieu'd
That in distresse had them so well rewarded:
   But Pride is scornd, contemnd, disdaind, derided,
   Whilst Humblenes of all things is prouided.

Oh then be humble, gentle, meeke, and milde;
So shalt thou be of euery mouth commended;
Be not disdainfull, cruell, proud, (sweet childe)
So shalt thou be of no man much condemned;
   Care not for them that Vertue doo despise;
   Vertue is loathde of fooles; loude of the wise.

O faire Boy trust not to thy Beauties wings,
They cannot carry thee aboue the Sunne:
Beauty and wealth are transitory things,
(For all must ende that euer was begunne)
    But Fame and Vertue neuer shall decay;
    For Fame is toombles, Vertue liues for aye.

The snow is white, and yet the pepper's blacke,
The one is bought, the other is contemned:
Pibbles we haue, but store of Ieat we lacke;
So white comparde to blacke is much condemned:
    We doo not praise the Swanne because shees white,
    But for she doth in Musique much delite.

And yet the siluer-noted Nightingale,
Though she be not so white is more esteemed;
Sturgion is dun of hew, white is the Whale,
Yet for the daintier Dish the first is deemed;
    What thing is whiter than the milke-bred Lilly?
    Thou knowes it not for naught, what man so silly?

Yea what more noysomer vnto the smell
Than Lillies are? what's sweeter than the Sage?
Yet for pure white the Lilly beares the Bell
Till it be faded through decaying Age;
    House-Doues are white, and Oozels Blacke-birds bee;
    Yet what a difference in the taste, we see.

Compare the Cow and Calfe, with Ewe and Lambe;
Rough hayrie Hydes, with softest downy Fell;
Hecfar and Bull, with Weather and with Ramme,
And you shall see how far they doo excell;
    White Kine with blacke, blacke Coney-skins with gray,
    Kine, nesh and strong; skin, deare and cheape alway.

The whitest siluer is not alwaies best,
Lead, Tynne, and Pewter are of base esteeme;
The yellow burnisht gold, that comes from th'East,
And West (of late inuented), may beseeme
    The worlds ritch Treasury, or *Mydas* eye;
    (The Ritch mans God, poore mans felicitie.)

Bugle and Ieat, with snow and Alablaster
I will compare: White Dammasin with blacke;
Bullas and wheaton Plumbs, (to a good Taster,)
The ripe red Cherries haue the sweetest smacke;
   When they be greene and young, th'are sowre and naught;
   But being ripe, with eagerness th'are baught.

Compare the Wyld-cat to the brownish Beauer,
Running for life, with hounds pursued sore;
When Hunts-men of her pretious Stones bereaue her
(Which with her teeth sh'had bitten off before):
   Restoratiues, and costly curious Felts
   Are made of them, and rich imbroydred Belts.

To what vse serues a peece of crimbling Chalke?
The Agget stone is white, yet good for nothing:
Fie, fie, I am asham'd to heare thee talke;
Be not so much of thine owne Image doating:
   So faire *Narcissus* lost his loue and life.
   (Beautie is often with itselfe at strife).

Right Diamonds are of a russet hieu,
The brightsome Carbuncles are red to see too,
The Saphyre stone is of a watchet blue,
(To this thou canst not chuse but soone agree too):
   Pearles are not white but gray, Rubies are red:
   In praise of Blacke, what can be better sed?

For if we doo consider of each mortall thing
That flyes in welkin, or in waters swims,
How euerie thing increaseth with the Spring,
And how the blacker still the brighter dims:
   We cannot chuse, but needs we must confesse,
   Sable excels milk-white in more or lesse.

As for example, in the christall cleare
Of a sweete streame, or pleasant running Riuer,
Where thousand formes of fishes will appeare,
(Whose names to thee I cannot now deliuer:)
   The blacker still the brighter haue disgrac'd,
   For pleasant profit, and delicious taste.

Salmon and Trout are of a ruddie colour,
Whiting and Dare is of a milk-white hiew:
Nature by them (perhaps) is made the fuller,
Little they nourish, be they old or new:
   Carp, Loach, Tench, Eeles (though black and bred in mud)
   Delight the tooth with taste, and breed good blud.

Innumerable be the kindes, if I could name them;
But I a Shepheard, and no Fisher am:
Little it skills whether I praise or blame them,
I onely meddle with my Ew and Lamb:
   Yet this I say, that blacke the better is,
   In birds, beasts, frute, stones, flowres, herbs, mettals, fish.

And last of all, in blacke there doth appeare
Such qualities, as not in yuorie;
Black cannot blush for shame, looke pale for fear,
Scorning to weare another liuorie.
   Blacke is the badge of sober Modestie,
   The wonted weare of ancient Grauetie.

The learned Sisters sute themselues in blacke,
Learning abandons white, and lighter hues:
Pleasure and Pride light colours neuer lacke;
But true Religion doth such Toyes refuse:
   Vertue and Grauity are sisters growne,
   Since blacke by both, and both by blacke are knowne.

White is the colour of each paltry Miller,
White is the Ensigne of each comman Woman;
White, is white Vertues for blacke Vyces Piller;
White makes proud fooles inferiour vnto no man:
   White, is the white of Body, blacke of Minde,
   (Vertue we seldome in white Habit finde.)

Oh then be not so proud because th'art fayre,
Vertue is onely the ritch gift of God:
Let not selfe-pride thy vertues name impayre,
Beate not greene youth with sharpe Repentance Rod:
   (A Fiend, a Monster, and mishapen Diuel;
   Vertues foe, Vyces friend, the roote of euill.)

Apply thy minde to be a vertuous man,
Auoyd ill company (the spoyle of youth;)
To follow Vertues Lore doo what thou can
(Whereby great profit vnto thee ensu[e]th :)
   Reade Bookes, hate Ignorance, (the foe to Art,
   The Damme of Errour, Enuy of the hart).

Serue *Ioue* (vpon thy knees) both day and night,
Adore his Name aboue all things on Earth :
So shall thy vowes be gracious in his sight,
So little Babes are blessed in their Birth :
   Thinke on no worldly woe, lament thy sin ;
   (For lesser cease, when greater griefes begin).

Sweare no vaine oathes ; heare much, but little say ;
Speake ill of no man, tend thine owne affaires,
Bridle thy wrath, thine angrie mood delay ;
(So shall thy minde be seldome cloyd with cares :)
   Be milde and gentle in thy speech to all,
   Refuse no honest gaine when it doth fall.

Be not beguild with words, proue not vngratefull,
Releeue thy Neighbour in his greatest need,
Commit no action that to all is hatefull,
Their want with welth, the poore with plentie feed:
   Twit no man in the teeth with what th'hast done ;
   Remember flesh is fraile, and hatred shunne.

Leaue wicked things, which Men to mischiefe moue,
(Least crosse mis-hap may thee in danger bring,)
Craue no preferment of thy heauenly *Ioue*,
Nor anie honor of thy earthly King :
   Boast not thy selfe before th'Almighties sight,
   (Who knowes thy hart, and anie wicked wight).

Be not offensiue to the peoples eye,
See that thy praiers harts true zeale affords,
Scorne not a man that's falne in miserie,
Esteeme no tatling tales, nor babling words ;
   That reason is exiled alwaies thinke,
   When as a drunkard rayles amidst his drinke.

THE AFFECTIONATE [R. Barnfield. Nov. 1594.

Vse not thy louely lips to loathsome lyes,
By craftie meanes increase no worldly wealth;
Striue not with mightie Men (whose fortune flies)
With temp'rate diet nourish wholesome health:
   Place well thy words, leaue not thy frend for gold;
   First trie, then trust; in ventring be not bold.

In *Pan* repose thy trust; extoll his praise
(That neuer shall decay, but euer liues):
Honor thy Parents (to prolong thy dayes),
Let not thy left hand know what right hand giues:
   From needie men turn not thy face away,
   (Though Charitie be now yclad in clay).

Heare Shepheards oft (thereby great wisdome growes),
With good aduice a sober answere make:
Be not remoou'd with euery winde that blowes,
(That course doo onely sinfull sinners take).
   Thy talke will shew thy fame or els thy shame;
   (As pratling tongue doth often purchase blame).

Obtaine a faithfull frend that will not faile thee,
Thinke on thy Mothers paine in her child-bearing,
Make no debate, least quickly thou bewaile thee,
Visit the sicke with comfortable chearing:
   Pittie the prisner, helpe the fatherlesse,
   Reuenge the Widdowes wrongs in her distresse.

Thinke on thy graue, remember still thy end,
Let not thy winding-sheete be staind with guilt,
Trust not a fained reconciled frend,
More than an open foe (that blood hath spilt)
   (Who tutcheth pitch, with pitch shalbe defiled),
   Be not with wanton companie beguiled.

Take not a flattring woman to thy wife,
A shameles creature, full of wanton words,
(Whose bad, thy good; whose lust will end thy life,
Cutting thy hart with sharpe two edged swords:)
   Cast not thy minde on her whose lookes allure,
   But she that shines in Truth and Vertue pure.

Praise not thy selfe, let other men commend thee;
Beare not a flattring tongue to glauer anie,
Let Parents due correction not offend thee:
Rob not thy neighbor, seeke the loue of manie;
   Hate not to heare good Counsell giuen thee,
   Lay not thy money vnto Vsurie.

Restraine thy steps from too much libertie,
Fulfill not th'enuious mans malitious minde;
Embrace thy Wife, liue not in lecherie;
Content thyselfe with what Fates haue assignde:
   Be rul'd by Reason, Warning dangers saue;
   True Age is reuerend worship to thy graue.

Be patient in extreame Aduersitie,
(Man's chiefest credit growes by dooing well,)
Be no high-minded in Prosperity;
Falshood abhorre, nor lying fable tell.
   Giue not thy selfe to Sloth, (the sinke of Shame,
   The moath of Time, the enemie to Fame.)

This leare I learned of a Bel-dame Trot,
(When I was yong and wylde as now thou art):
But her good counsell I regarded not;
I markt it with my eares, not with my hart:
   But now I finde it too–too true (my Sonne),
   When my Age-withered Spring is almost done.

Behold my gray head, full of siluer haires,
My wrinckled skin, deepe furrowes in my face:
Cares bring Old-Age, Old-Age increaseth cares;
My Time is come, and I haue run my Race:
   Winter hath snow'd vpon my hoarie head,
   And with my Winter all my ioys are dead.

And thou loue-hating Boy, (whom once I loued),
Farewell, a thousand-thousand times farewell;
My Teares the Marble Stones to ruth haue moued;
My sad Complaints the babling Ecchoes tell:
   And yet thou wouldst take no compassion on mee,
   Scorning that crosse which Loue hath laid vpon mee.

The hardest steele with fier doth mend his misse,
Marble is mollifyde with drops of Raine;
But thou (more hard than Steele or Marble is)
Doost scorne my Teares, and my true loue disdaine,
    Which for thy sake shall euerlasting bee,
    Wrote in the Annalls of Eternitie.

By this, the Night (with darknes ouer-spred)
Had drawne the curtaines of her cole-blacke bed;
And *Cynthia* muffling her face with a clowd,
(Lest all the world of her should be too prowd)
    Had taken *Conge* of the sable Night,
    (That wanting her cannot be halfe so bright;)

When I poore forlorne man and outcast creature
(Despairing of my Loue, despisde of Beautie)
Grew male-content, scorning his louely feature,
That had disdaind my euer-zealous dutie:
    I hy'd me homeward by the Moone-shine light;
    Forswearing Loue, and all his fond delight.

FINIS.

The Shepherds Content
OR
The happines of a harmless life.

Written upon Occasion of the

former Subject.

OF all the kindes of common Countrey life,
    Me thinkes a Shepheards life is most Content;
    His State is quiet Peace, deuoyd of strife;
    His thoughts are pure from all impure intent,
    His Pleasures rate sits at an easie rent:
      He beares no mallice in his harmles hart,
      Malicious meaning hath in him no part.

He is not troubled with th'afflicted minde,
His cares are onely ouer silly Sheepe;
He is not vnto Iealozie inclinde,
(Thrice happie Man) he knowes not how to weepe;
Whil'st I the Treble in deepe sorrowes keepe;
  I cannot keepe the Meane; for why (alas)
  Griefes haue no meane, though I for meane doe passe.

No Briefes nor Semi-Briefes are in my Songs,
Because (alas) my griefe is seldome shoot;
My Prick-Song's alwayes full of Largues and Longs,
(Because I neuer can obtaine the Port
Of my desires: Hope is a happie Fort.)
  Prick-song (indeed) because it pricks my hart;
  And Song, because sometimes I ease my smart.

CONTENT.

[R. Barnfield.
Nov. 1594.

The mightie Monarch of a royall Realme,
Swaying his Scepter with a Princely pompe ;
Of his desires cannot so steare the Healme,
But sometime falls into a deadly dumpe,
When as he heares the shrilly-sounding Trumpe
   Of Forren Enemies, or home-bred Foes ;
   His minde of griefe, his hart is full of woes.

Or when bad subiects gainst their Soueraigne
(Like hollow harts) vnnaturally rebell,
How carefull is he to suppresse againe
Their desperate forces, and their powers to quell
With loyall harts, till all (againe) be well :
   When (being subdu'd) his care is rather more
   To keepe them vnder, than it was before.

Thus is he neuer full of sweete Content,
But either this or that his ioy debars :
Now Noble-men gainst Noble-men are bent,
Now Gentlemen and others fall at iarrs :
Thus is his Countrey full of ciuill warrs ;
   He still in danger sits, still fearing Death :
   For Traitors seeke to stop their Princes breath.

The whylst the other hath no enemie,
Without it be the Wolfe and cruell Fates
(Which no man spare) : when as his disagree
He with his sheep-hooke knaps them on the pates,
Schooling his tender Lambs from wanton gates :
   Beasts are more kinde then Men, Sheepe seeke not blood
   But countrey caytiues kill their Countreyes good.

The Courtier he fawn's for his Princes fauour,
In hope to get a Princely ritch Reward ;
His tongue is tipt with honey for to glauer ;
Pride deales the Deck whilst Chance doth choose the Card,
Then comes another and his Game hath mard ;
   Sitting betwixt him, and the morning Sun :
   Thus Night is come before the Day is done.

Some Courtiers carefull of their Princes health,
Attends his Person with all dilligence
Whose hand's their hart ; whose welfare is their wealth,
Whose safe Protection is their sure Defence,
For pure affection, not for hope of pence :
    Such is the faithfull hart, such is the minde,
    Of him that is to Vertue still inclinde.

The skilfull Scholler, and braue man at Armes,
First plies his Booke, last fights for Countries Peace;
Th'one feares Obliuion, th'other fresh Alarmes ;
His paines nere ende, his trauailes neuer cease ;
His with the Day, his with the Night increase :
    He studies how to get eternall Fame ;
    The Souldier fights to win a glorious Name.

The Knight, the Squire, the Gentleman, the Clowne,
Are full of crosses and calamities ;
Lest fickle Fortune should begin to frowne,
And turne their mirth to extreame miseries :
Nothing more certaine than incertainties ;
    Fortune is full of fresh varietie :
    Constant in nothing but inconstancie.

The wealthie Merchant that doth crosse the Seas,
To *Denmarke, Poland, Spaine,* and *Barbarie;*
For all his ritches, liues not still at ease ;
Sometimes he feares ship-spoyling Pyracie,
Another while deceipt and treacherie
    Of his owne Factors in a forren Land ;
    Thus doth he still in dread and danger stand.

Well is he tearmd a Merchant-Venturer,
Since he doth venter lands, and goods, and all :
When he doth trauell for his Traffique far,
Little he knowes what fortune may befall,
Or rather what mis-fortune happen shall :
    Sometimes he splits his Ship against a rocke ;
    Loosing his men, his goods, his wealth, his stocke.

And if he so escape with life away,
He counts himselfe a man most fortunate,
Because the waues their rigorous rage did stay,
(When being within their cruell powers of late,
The Seas did seeme to pittie his estate)
    But yet he neuer can recouer health,
    Because his ioy was drowned with his wealth.

The painfull Plough-swaine, and the Husband-man
Rise vp each morning by the breake of day,
Taking what toyle and drudging paines they can,
And all is for to get a little stay;
And yet they cannot put their care away:
    When Night is come, their cares begin afresh,
    Thinking vpon their Morrowes busines.

Thus euerie man is troubled with vnrest,
From rich to poore, from high to low degree:
Therefore I thinke that man is truly blest,
That neither cares for wealth nor pouertie,
But laughs at Fortune and her foolerie;
    That giues rich Churles great store of golde and fee,
    And lets poore Schollers liue in miserie,

O fading Branches of decaying Bayes
Who now will water your dry-wither'd Armes?
Or where is he that sung the louely Layes
Of simple Shepheards in their Countrey-Farmes?
Ah he is dead, the cause of all our harmes:
    And with him dide my ioy and sweete delight:
    And cleare to Clowdes, the Day is turnd to Night.

SYDNEY. The Syren of this latter Age;
SYDNEY. The Blasing-starre of England's glory;
SYDNEY. The Wonder of wise and sage;
SYDNEY. The Subiect of true Vertues story;
    This Syren, Starre, this Wonder, and this Subiect;
    In dumbe, dim, gone, and mard by Fortunes Obiect.

And thou my sweete *Amintas* vertuous minde,
Should I forget thy Learning or thy Loue;
Well might I be accounted but vnkinde,
Whose pure affection I so oft did proue:
Might my poore Plaints hard stones to pitty moue;
 His losse should be lamented of each Creature,
 So great his Name, so gentle was his Nature.

But sleepe his soule in sweet Elysium,
(The happy Hauen of eternall rest:)
And let me to my former matter come,
Prouing by Reason, Shepheard's life is best,
Because he harbours Vertue in his Brest;
 And is content (the chiefest thing of all)
 With any fortune that shall him befall.

He sits all Day lowd-piping on a Hill,
The whilst his flocke about him daunce apace,
His hart with ioy, his eares with Musique fill:
Anon a bleating Weather beares the Bace,
A Lambe the Treble; and to his disgrace
 Another answers like a middle Meane:
 Thus euery one to beare a Part are faine.

Like a great King he rules a little Land,
Still making Statutes, and ordayning Lawes;
Which if they breake, he beates them with his Wand:
He doth defend them from the greedy Iawes
Of rau'ning Wooluěs, and Lyons bloudy Pawes.
 His Field, his Realme; his Subiects are his Sheepe;
 Which he doth still in due obedience keepe.

First he ordaines by Act of Parlament,
(Holden by custome in each Countrey Towne),
That if a sheepe (with any bad intent)
Presume to breake the neighbour Hedges downe,
Or haunt strange Pastures that be not his owne;
 He shall be pounded for his lustines,
 Vntill his Master finde out some redres.

Also if any proue a Strageller
From his owne fellowes in a forraine field,
He shall be taken for a wanderer,
And forc'd himselfe immediatly to yeeld,
Or with a wyde-mouth'd Mastiue Curre be kild.
  And if not claimd within a twelue-month's space,
  He shall remaine with Land-lord of the place.

Or if one stray to feede far from the rest,
He shall be pincht by his swift pye-bald Curre;
If any by his fellowes be opprest,
The wronger (for he doth all wrong abhorre)
Shall be well bangd so long as he can sturre.
  Because he did anoy his harmeles Brother,
  That meant not harme to him nor any other.

And last of all, if any wanton Weather,
With briers and brambles teare his fleece in twaine,
He shall be forc'd t'abide cold frosty weather,
And powring showres of ratling stormes of raine,
Till his new fleece begins to grow againe:
  And for his rashnes he is doom'd to goe
  without a new Coate all the Winter throw.

Thus doth he keepe them, still in awfull feare,
And yet allowes them liberty inough;
So deare to him their welfare doth appeare,
That when their fleeces gin to waxen rough,
He combs and trims them with a Rampicke bough,
  Washing them in the streames of siluer *Ladon*,
  To cleanse their skinnes from all corruption.

Another while he wooes his Country Wench,
(With Chaplets crownd, and gaudy girlonds dight)
Whose burning Lust her modest eye doth quench,
Standing amazed at her heauenly sight,
(Beauty doth rauish Sense with sweet Delight)
  Clearing *Arcadia* with a smoothed Browe
  When Sun-bright smiles melts flakes of driuen snowe.

Thus doth he frollicke it each day by day,
And when Night comes drawes homeward to his Coate,
Singing a Iigge or merry Roundelay ;
(For who sings commonly so merry a Noate,
As he that cannot chop or change a groate)
   And in the winter Nights (his chiefe desire)
   He turns a Crabbe or Cracknell in the fire.

He leads his Wench a Country Horn-pipe Round,
About a May-pole on a Holy-day ;
Kissing his louely Lasse (with Garlands Crownd)
With whoopping heigh-ho singing Care away ;
Thus doth he passe the merry month of May :
   And all th'yere after in delight and ioy,
   (Scorning a King) he cares for no annoy.

What though with simple cheere he homely fares?
He liues content, a King can doo no more ;
Nay not so much, for Kings haue manie cares :
But he hath none ; except it be that sore
Which yong and old, which vexeth ritch and poore,
   The pangs of Loue. O ! who can vanquish Loue?
   That conquers Kingdomes, and the Gods aboue?

Deepe-wounding Arrow, hart-consuming Fire ;
Ruler of Reason, slaue to tyraunt Beautie ;
Monarch of harts, Fuell of fond desire,
Prentice to Folly, foe to faind Duetie.
Pledge of true Zeale, Affections moitie ;
   If thou kilst where thou wilt, and whom it list thee,
   (Alas) how can a silly Soule resist thee ?

By thee great *Collin* lost his libertie,
By thee sweet *Astrophel* forwent his ioy ;
By thee *Amyntas* wept incessantly,
By thee good *Rowland* liu'd in great annoy ;
O cruell, peeuish, vylde, blind-seeing Boy :
   How canst thou hit their harts, and yet not see ?
   (If thou be blinde, as thou art faind to bee).

THE SHEPHEARDS [R. Barnfield. Nov. 1594.

A Shepheard loues no ill, but onely thee;
He hath no care, but onely by thy causing:
Why doost thou shoot thy cruell shafts at mee?
Giue me some respite, some short time of pausing:
Still my sweet Loue with bitter lucke th'art sawcing:
  Oh, if thou hast a minde to shew thy might;
  Kill mightie Kings, and not a wretched wight.

Yet (O Enthraller of infranchizd harts)
At my poor hart if thou wilt needs be ayming,
Doo me the fauour, show me both thy Darts,
That I may chuse the best for my harts mayming,
(A free consent is priuiledgd from blaming:)
  Then pierce his hard hart with thy golden Arrow,
  That thou my wrong, that he may rue my sorrow.

But let mee feele the force of thy lead Pyle,
What should I doo with loue when I am old?
I know not how to flatter, fawne, or smyle;
Then stay thy hand, O cruell Bow-man hold:
For if thou strik'st me with thy dart of gold,
  I sweare to thee (by Ioues immortall curse)
  I haue more in my hart, than in my purse.

The more I weepe, the more he bends his Bow,
For in my hart a golden Shaft I finde:
(Cruell, vnkinde) and wilt thou leaue me so?
Can no remorce nor pittie moue thy minde?
Is Mercie in the Heauens so hard to finde?
  Oh, then it is no meruaile that on earth
  Of kinde Remorce there is so great a dearth.

How happie were a harmles Shepheards life,
If he had neuer knowen what Loue did meane;
But now fond Loue in euery place is rife,
Staining the purest Soule with spots vncleane,
Making thicke purses, thin: and fat bodies, leane:
  Loue is a fiend, a fire, a heauen, a hell;
  Where pleasure, paine, and sad repentance dwell.

There are so manie *Danaes* nowadayes,
That loue for lucre; paine for gaine is sold:
No true affection can their fancie please,
Except it be a *Ioue*, to raine downe gold
Into their laps, which they wyde open hold:
  If *legem pone* comes, he is receau'd,
  When *Vix haud habeo* is of hope bereau'd.

Thus haue I showed in my Countrey vaine
The sweet Content that Shepheards still inioy;
The mickle pleasure, and the little paine
That euer doth awayte the Shepheards Boy:
His hart is neuer troubled with annoy.
  He is a King, for he commands his Sheepe;
  He knowes no woe, for he doth seldome weepe.

He is a Courtier, for he courts his Loue:
He is a Scholler, for he sings sweet Ditties:
He is a Souldier, for he wounds doth proue;
He is the fame of Townes, the shame of Citties;
He scornes false Fortune, put true Vertue pitties.
  He is a Gentleman, because his nature
  Is kinde and affable to euerie Creature.

Who would not then a simple Shepheard bee,
Rather than be a mightie Monarch made?
Since he inioyes such perfect libertie,
As neuer can decay, nor neuer fade:
He seldome sits in dolefull Cypresse shade;
  But liues in hope, in ioy, in peace, in blisse:
  Ioying all ioy with this content of his.

But now good-fortune lands my little Boate
Vpon the shoare of his desired rest:
Now I must leaue (awhile) my rurall noate,
To thinke on him whom my soule loueth best;
He that can make the most vnhappie blest:
  In whose sweete lap Ile lay me downe to sleepe,
  And neuer wake till Marble-stones shall weepe.

FINIS.

SONNET.

Oe here behold these tributarie Teares
Paid to thy faire, but cruell tyrant Eyes;
Loe here the blossome of my youthfull yeares,
Nipt with the fresh of thy Wraths winter, dyes,

Here on Loues Altar I doo offer vp
This burning hart for my Soules sacrifice;
Here I receaue this deadly-poysned Cu[p]
Of *Circe* charm'd; wherein deepe Magicke lyes.

Then Teares (if thou be happie Teares indeed),
And Hart (if thou be lodged in his brest),
And Cup (if thou canst helpe despaire with speed);
Teares, Hart, and Cup conjoyne to make me blest:
  Teares moue, Hart win, Cup cause, ruth, loue, desire,
  In word, in deed, by moane, by zeale, by fire.

FINIS.

THE COMPLAINT
OF CHASTITIE.

Briefely touching the cause of the death of *Matilda Fitzwalters* an English Ladie; sometime loued of King *Iohn*, after poysoned. The Storie is at large written by *Michael Dreyton*.

Ou modest Dames, inricht with Chastitie.
  Maske your bright eyes with *Vestaes* sable Vaile,
Since few are left so faire or chast as shee;
(Matter for me to weepe, you to bewaile):
For manie seeming so, of Vertue faile;
  Whose louely Cheeks (with rare vermillion tainted)
  Can neuer blush because their faire is painted.

O faire-foule Tincture, staine of Woman-kinde,
Mother of Mischiefe, Daughter of Deceate,
False traitor to the Soule, blot to the Minde,
Vsurping Tyrant of true Beauties seate,
Right Cousner of the eye, lewd Follies baite,
  The flag of filthines, the sinke of shame,
  The Diuells dye, dishonour of thy name.

THE COMPLAINT

[R. Barnfield. Nov. 1594.

Monster of Art, Bastard of bad Desier,
Il-worshipt Idoll, false Imagerie,
Ensigne of Vice, to thine owne selfe a lier,
Silent Inchaunter, mindes Anatomie,
Sly Bawd to Lust, Pandor to Infamie,
   Slaunder of Truth, Truth of Dissimulation;
   Staining our Clymate more than anie Nature.

What shall I say to thee? thou scorne of Nature,
Blacke spot of sinne, vylde lure of lecherie;
Iniurious Blame to euerie faemale creature,
Wronger of time, Broker of trecherie,
Trap of greene youth, false Womens witcherie,
   Hand-maid of pride, high-way to wickednesse;
   Yet path-way to Repentance, nere the lesse.

Thou dost entice the minde to dooing euill,
Thou setst dissention twixt the man and wife;
A Saint in show, and yet indeed a deuill:
Thou art the cause of euerie common strife;
Thou art the life of Death, the death of Life!
   Thou doost betray thyselfe to Infamie,
   When thou art once discernd by the eye.

Ah, little knew *Matilda* of thy being,
Those times were pure from all impure complection;
Then Loue came at Desert, Desert of seeing,
Then Vertue was the mother of Affection,
(But Beautie now is vnder no subiection),
   Then women were the same that men did deeme,
   But now they are the same they doo not seeme.

What fæmale now intreated of a King
With gold and iewels, pearles and precious stones,
Would willingly refuse so sweete a thing?
Onely for a little show of Vertue ones?
Women haue kindnes grafted in their bones.
   Gold is a deepe-perswading Orator,
   Especially where few the fault abhor.

But yet shee rather deadly poyson chose,
(Oh cruell Bane of most accursed Clime;)
Than staine that milk-white Mayden-virgin Rose,
Which shee had kept vnspotted till that time:
And not corrupted with this earthly slime
  Her soule shall liue: inclosd eternally,
  In that pure shrine of Immortality.

This is my Doome: and this shall come to passe,
For what are Pleasures but still-vading ioyes?
Fading as flowers, brittle as a glasse,
Or Potters Clay; crost with the least annoyes;
All thinges in this life are but trifling Toyes:
  But Fame and Vertue neuer shall decay,
  For Fame is Toomblesse, Vertue liues for aye!

FINIS.

Hellens Rape.

OR

A light Lanthorne for light Ladies.

Written in English Hexameters.

Ouely a Lasse, so loued a Lasse, and (alas) such a louing
Lasse, for a while (but a while) was none such a sweet bonny Loue-Lasse
As Helen, Mænelaus louing, lou'd, loulie a loue-lasse,
Till spightfull Fortune from a loue-lasse made her a loue-lesse
Wife. From a wise woman to a witles vvanton abandond,
When her mate (vnawares) made warres in Peloponessus,
Adultrous Paris (then a Boy) kept sheepe as a shepheard
On Ida Mountaine, vnknowne to the King for a Keeper
Of sheep, on Ida Mountaine, as a Boy, as a shepheard:
Yet such sheep he kept, and was so seemelie a shepheard,
Seemlie a Boy, so seemlie a youth, so seemlie a Younker,
That on Ida was not such a Boy, such a youth, such a Younker.
Sonne now reconcil'd to the Father, fained a letter
Sent him by Iupiter (the greatest God in Olympus)
For to repaire with speede to the brauest Græcian Hauen,

And to redeeme againe Hesyone *latelie reuolted*
From Troy *by* Aiax, *whom she had newly betrothed.*
Well, so well he told his tale to his Aunt Amaryllis
That Amaryllis, *(his Aunt,) obtaind aid of his aged*
Syre, that he sent him a ship, and made Capten of Argus.
Great store went to Greece with lust-bewitched Alexis,
Telamour, *and* Tydias : *with these he sliceth the salt seas,*
The salt seas slicing, at length he comes to the firme land,
Firme land an auntient Iland cald old Lacedæmon.
Argus *(eye full Earle) when first the ken of a Castle*
He had spide bespake : (to the Mate, to the men, to the Mates-man,
Lo behold of Greece (quoth he) the great Cytadella.
(Ycleaped Menela*) so tearmed of* Deliaes *Husband :*
Happie Helen, *Womens most woonder, beautifull* Helen.
Oh would God (quoth he) with a flattring Tongue he repeated :
Oh would God (quoth he) that I might deserue to be husband
To such a happie huswife, to such a beautifull Helen.
This he spake to intice the minde of a lecherous young-man :
But what spurres need now, for an vntam'd Titt to be trotting :
Or to add old Oile to the flame, new flaxe to the fier :
Paris *heard him hard, and gaue good eare to his hearkening :*
And then his loue to a lust, his lust was turnd to a fier,
Fier was turnd to a flame, and flame was turnd to a burning
Brand : and mothers Dreame was then most truelie resolued.
Well so far th'are come, that now th'are come to the Castle,
Castle all of stone, yet euery stone vvas a Castle :
Euerie foote had a Fort, and euerie Fort had a fountaine,
Euerie fountaine a spring, and euerie spring had a spurting
Streame : so strong without, vvithin, so stately a building,
Neuer afore vvas seene ; If neuer afore Polyphœbe
Was seene : vvas to be seene, if nere to be seene vvas Olympus.
Flovvers vvere framd of flints, Walls, Rubies, Rafters of Argent :
Pauement of Chrisolite, Windows contriu'd of a Cristall :
Vessels were of gold, with gold was each thing adorned :
Golden Webs more worth than a vvealthy Souldan *of* Egypt,
And her selfe more vvorth than a vvealthy Souldan *of* Egypt :

And her selfe more worth than all the wealth shee possessed;
Selfe? indeede such a selfe, as thundring Ioue *in* Olympus,
Though he were father could finde in his hart to be husband.
Embassage ended, to the Queene of faire Lacedæmon;
(Happie King of a Queene so faire, of a Countrey so famous)
Embassage ended, a Banquet braue was appointed:
Sweet Repast for a Prince, fine Iunkets fit for a Kings sonne.
Biskets and Carrawayes, Comfets, Tart, Plate, Ielley, Ginger-bread,
Lymons and Medlars: and Dishes moe by a thousand.
First they fell to the feast, and after fall to a Dauncing,
And from a Dance to a Trance, from a Trance they fell to a falling,
Either in other armes, and either in armes of another.
Pastime ouer-past, and Banquet duely prepared,
Deuoutly pared: Each one hies home to his owne home,
Saue Lord and Ladie; Young Lad, but yet such an old Lad,
In such a Ladies lappe, at such a slipperie by-blow,
That in a vvorld so vvilde, could not be found such a wilie
Lad: in an Age so old, could not be found such an old lad:
Old lad, and bold lad, such a Boy, such a lustie Iuuentus:
Well to their vvorke they goe, and both they iumble in one Bed:
Worke so well they like, that they still like to be vvorking:
For Aurora *mounts before he leaues to be mounting:*
And Astræa *fades before she faints to be falling:*
*(*Helen *a light Huswife, now a lightsome starre in* Olympus.)

FINIS.

Cynthia.
VVITH CER-
taine Sonnets, and
the Legend of
Cassandra.

Quod cupio nequeo.

At London,
Printed for Humfrey
Lownes, and are to bee
sold at the VVest doore
of Paules. 1595.

To the Right Honorable, and
most noble-minded Lorde,
William Stanley, Earle of Darby, &c.

Ight Honorable, the dutifull affection I beare to your manie vertues, is cause, that to manifest my loue to your Lordship, I am constrained to shew my simplenes to the world. Many are they that admire your worth, of the which number, I (though the meanest in abilitie, yet with the formost in affection) am one that most desire to serue, and onely to serue your Honour.

Small is the gift, but great is my good-will; the which, by how much the lesse I am able to expresse it, by so much the more it is infinite. Liue long: and inherit your Predecessors vertues, as you doe their dignitie and estate. This is my wish: the which your honorable excellent giftes doe promise me to obtaine: and whereof these few rude and vnpollished lines, are a true (though an vndeseruing) testimony. If my ability were better, the signes should be greater; but being as it is, your honour must take me as I am, not as I should be. My yeares being so young, my perfection cannot be greater: But howsoeuer it is, yours it is; and I my selfe am yours; in all humble seruice, most ready to be commaunded.

Richard Barnefeilde.

To the curteous Gentlemen Readers.

GEntlemen; the last Terme [*i.e., November* 1594] there came forth a little toy of mine, intituled, *The affectionate Shepheard*: In the which, his Country *Content* found such friendly fauor, that it hath incouraged me to publish my second fruites. *The affectionate Shepheard* being the first: howsoeuer undeseruedly (I protest) I haue beene thought (of some) to haue beene the authour of two Books heretofore. I neede not to name them, because they are two-well knowne already: nor will I deny them, because they are dislik't; but because they are not mine. This protestation (I hope) will satisfie th'indifferent: as for them that are maliciously enuious, as I cannot, so I care not to please. Some there were, that did interpret *The affectionate Shepheard*, otherwise then (in truth) I meant, touching the subiect thereof, to wit, the loue of a Shepheard to a boy; a fault, the which I will not excuse, because I neuer made. Onely this, I will vnshaddow my conceit: being nothing else, but an imitation of *Virgill*, in the second Eglogue of *Alexis*. In one or two places (in this Booke) I vse the name of *Eliza* pastorally: wherein, lest any one should misconster my meaning (as I hope none will) I haue here briefly discouered my harmeles conceipt as concerning that name: whereof once (in a simple Shepheards deuice) I wrot this Epigramme.

> *One name there is, which name aboue all other*
> *I most esteeme, as time and place shall proue:*
> *The one is* Vesta, *th'other* Cupids *Mother,*
> *The first my Goddesse is, the last my loue;*
>   *Subiect to Both I am: to that by berth;*
>   *To this for beautie; fairest on the earth.*

Thus, hoping you will beare with my rude conceit of *Cynthia*, (if for no other cause, yet, for that it is the first imitation of the verse of that excellent Poet, Maister *Spencer*, in his *Fayrie Queene*) I will leaue you to the reading of that, which I so much desire may breed your Delight.

                                        Richard Barnefeild.

T. T. in commendation of the *Authour his worke.*

Whylom that in a shepheards gray coate masked,
(Where masked loue the nonage of his skill)
Reares new Eagle-winged pen, new tasked,
To scale the by-clift Muse sole-pleasing hill:
Dropping sweete Nectar poesie from his quill,
Admires faire C Y N T H I A with his iuory pen
Faire C Y N T H I A lou'd, fear'd, of Gods and men.

Downe sliding from that cloudes ore-pearing mounteine:
Decking with double grace the neighbour plaines, [fountain,
Drawes christall dew, from P E G A S E foote-sprung
Whose flower set banks, delights, sweet choice containes:
Nere yet discouerd to the country swaines:
   Heere bud those branches, which adorne his turtle,
   With loue made garlands, of heart-bleeding Mirtle.

Rays'd from the cynders, of the thrice-sact towne:
I L L I O N S sooth-telling S Y B I L L I S T appeares,
Eclipsing P H O E B U S loue, with scornefull frowne,
Whose tragicke end, affords warme-water teares,
(For pitty-wanting P A C O E, none forbeares)
   Such period haps, to beauties price ore-priz'd:
   Where I A N V S-faced loue, doth lurke disguiz'd.

Nere-waining C Y N T H I A yeelds thee triple thankes,
Whose beames vnborrowed darke the worlds faire eie
And as full streames that euer fill their bankes,
So those rare Sonnets, where wits ripe doth lie,
With Troian Nimph, doe soare thy fame to skie.
   And those, and these, contend thy Muse to raise
   (Larke mounting Muse) with more then common praise.

To his Mistresse.

Right Starre of Beauty, fairest Faire aliue,
  Rare president of peerelesse chastity;
(In whom the Muses and the Graces striue,
  VVhich shall possesse the chiefest part of thee:)
Oh let these simple lines accepted bee:
    VVhich here I offer at thy sacred shrine:
    Sacred, because sweet Beauty is diuine.

And though I cannot please each curious eare,
With sugred Noates of heauenly Harmonie:
Yet if my loue shall to thy selfe appeare,
No other Muse I will inuoke but thee:
And if thou wilt my faire *Thalia* be,
    Ile sing sweet Hymnes and praises to thy name,
    In that cleare Temple of eternall Fame.

But ah (alas) how can mine infant Muse
(That neuer heard of *Helicon* before)
Performe my promise past: when they refuse
Poore Shepheards Plaints? yet will I still adore
Thy sacred Name, al though I write no more:
    Yet hope I shall, if this accepted bee:
    If not, in silence sleepe eternally.

CYNTHIA.

Ow was the Welkyn all inuelloped
    With duskie Mantle of the sable Night:
    And CYNTHIA lifting vp her drouping head,
    Blusht at the Beautie of her borrowed light,
    When Sleepe now summon'd euery mortal wight.
Then loe (me thought) I saw or seem'd to see,
An heauenly Creature like an Angell bright,
  That in great haste came pacing towards me:
Was neuer mortall eye beheld so faire a Shee.

Thou lazie man (quoth she) what mak'st thou heere
  (Luld in the lap of Honours Enimie?)
  I heere commaund thee now for to appeare
  (By vertue of IOVES mickle Maiestie)
  In yonder Wood. (Which with her finger shee
Out-poynting) had no sooner turn'd her face,
And leauing mee to muze what she should bee,
  Vanished into some other place:
But straite (me thought) I saw a rout of heauenlie Race.

Downe in a Dale, hard by a Forrest side,
  (Vnder the shaddow of a loftie Pine,)
Not far from whence a trickling streame did glide,
Did nature by her secret art combine,
A pleasant Arbour, of a spreading Vine:
Wherein Art stroue with nature to compaire,
That made it rather seeme a thing diuine
Being scituate all in the open Aire:
A fairer nere was seene, if any seene so faire.

There might one see, and yet not see (indeede)
  Fresh *Flora* flourishing in chiefest Prime,
  Arrayed all in gay and gorgeous weede,
The Primrose and sweet-smelling Eglantine,
As fitted best beguiling so the time:
And euer as she went she strewd the place,
Red-roses mixt with Daffadillies fine,
For Gods and Goddesses, that in like case
In this same order sat, with il-beseeming grace.

First, in a royall Chaire of massie gold,
  (Bard all about with plates of burning steele)
Sat *Iupiter* most glorious to behold,
And in his hand was placed Fortunes wheele:
The which he often turn'd, and oft did reele.
And next to him, in griefe and gealouzie,
(If sight may censure what the heart doth feele)
In sad lament was placed *Mercurie*;
That dying seem'd to weep, and weeping seem'd to die.

On th'other side, aboue the other twaine,
  (Delighting as it seem'd to sit alone)
Sat *Mulciber*; in pride and high disdaine,
Mounted on high vpon a stately throne,
And euen with that I heard a deadly grone:
Muzing at this, and such an vncouth sight,
(Not knowing what shoulde make that piteous mone)
I saw three furies, all in Armour dight,
With euery one a Lampe, and euery one a light.

I deemed so; nor was I much deceau'd,
  For poured forth in sensuall Delight,
  There might I see of Sences quite bereau'd
King *Priams* Sonne, that *Alexander* hight
(Wrapt in the Mantle of eternall Night.)
And vnder him, awaiting for his fall,
  Sate Shame, here Death, and there sat fel Despight,
  That with their Horrour did his heart appall:
Thus was his Blisse to Bale, his Hony turn'd to gall.

In which delight feeding mine hungry eye,
  Of two great Goddesses a sight I had,
  And after them in wondrous Iollity,
(As one that inly ioy'd, so was she glad)
The Queene of Loue full royallie yclad,
In glistring Gold, and peerelesse precious stone,
  There might I spie: and her Companion had,
  Proud *Paris*, Nephew to *Laomedon*,
That afterward did cause the Death of many a one.

By this the formost melting all in teares,
  And rayning downe resolued Pearls in showers,
  Gan to approach the place of heauenly Pheares,
And with her weeping, watring all their Bowers,
Throwing sweet Odors on those fading flowers,
At length, she them bespake thus mournfullie.
  High *Ioue* (quoth she) and yee Cœlestiall powers,
  That here in Iudgement sit twixt her and mee,
Now listen (for a while) and iudge with equitie.

Sporting our selues to day, as wee were woont
  (I meane, I, *Pallas*, and the Queene of Loue.)
  Intending with *Diana* for to hunt,
On *Ida* Mountaine top our skill to proue,
A golden Ball was trindled from aboue,
And on the Rinde was writ this Poesie,
  PVLCHERIMÆ for which a while we stroue,
  Each saying shee was fairest of the three,
When loe a shepheards Swaine not far away we see.

I spi'd him first, and spying thus bespake,
  Shall yonder Swaine vnfolde the mysterie?
  Agreed (quoth *Venus*) and by *Stygian* Lake,
  To whom he giues the ball so shall it bee:
  Nor from his censure will I flie, quoth shee,
  (Poynting to *Pallas*) though I loose the gole.
  Thus euery one yplac'd in her degree,
    The Shepheard comes, whose partial eies gan role,
And on our beuties look't, and of our beuties stole.

I promis'd wealth, *Minerua* promised wit,
  (Shee promis'd wit to him that was vnwise,)
  But he (fond foole) had soone refused it,
  And minding to bestow that glorious Prize,
  On *Venus*, that with pleasure might suffize
  His greedie minde in loose lasciuiousnes:
  Vpon a sudden, wanting goode aduice,
    Holde heere (quoth he) this golden Ball possesse,
Which *Paris* giues to thee for meede of worthines,

Thus haue I shew'd the summe of all my sute,
  And as a Plaintiffe heere appeale to thee,
  And to the rest. Whose folly I impute
  To filthie lust, and partialitie,
  That made him iudge amisse: and so doo we
  (Quoth *Pallas*, *Venus*,) nor will I gaine-say,
  Although it's mine by right, yet willinglie,
    I heere disclaime my title and obey:
When silence being made, *Ioue* thus began to saie.

Thou *Venus*, art my darling, thou my deare,
  (*Minerua*,) shee, my sister and my wife:
  So that of all a due respect I beare,
  Assign'd as one to end this doubtfull strife,
  (Touching your forme, your fame, your loue, your life)
  Beauty is vaine much like a gloomy light,
  And wanting wit is counted but a trife,
    Especially when Honour's put to flight:
Thus of a louely, soone becomes a loathly sight.

WVit without wealth is bad, yet counted good,
  wealth wanting wisdom's worse, yet deem'd as wel,
  From whence (for ay) doth flow, as from a flood,
  A pleasant Poyson, and a heauenly Hell,
  where mortall men do couet still to dwell.
  Yet one there is to Vertue so inclin'd,
  That as for Maiesty she beares the Bell,
  So in the truth who tries her princelie minde,
Both Wisdom, Beauty, Wealth, and all in her shall find.

In Westerne world amids the Ocean maine,
  In compleat Vertue shining like the Sunne,
  In great Renowne a maiden Queene doth raigne,
  Whose royall Race, in Ruine first begun,
  Till Heauens bright Lamps dissolue shall nere be done:
  In whose faire eies Loue linckt with vertues been,
  In euerlasting Peace and Vnion.
  Which sweet Consort in her full well beseeme
Of Bounty, and of Beauty fairest Fayrie Queene.

And to conclude, the gifts in her yfound,
  Are all so noble, royall, and so rare,
  That more and more in her they doe abound;
  In her most peerelesse Prince without compare,
  Endowing still her minde with vertuous care:
  That through the world (so wide) the flying fame,
  (And Name that Enuies selfe cannot impaire,)
  Is blown of this faire Queen, this gorgeous dame,
Fame borrowing al men's mouths to royalize the same.

And with this sentence *Iupiter* did end,
  This is the Pricke (quoth he), this is the praies,
  To whom, this as a Present I will send,
  That shameth *Cynthia* in her siluer Raies,
  If so you three this deed doe not displease.
  Then one, and all, and euery one of them,
  To her that is the honour of her daies,
  A second *Iudith* in I E R V S A L E M.
To her we send this Pearle, this Iewell, and this Iem.

Then call'd he vp the winged *Mercury*,
  (The mighty Messenger of Gods enrold,)
And bad him hither hastily to hie,
Whom tended by her Nymphes he should behold,
  (Like Pearles ycouched all in shining gold.)
And euen with that, from pleasant slumbring sleepe,
  (Desiring much these wonders to vnfold)
I wak'ning, when *Aurora* gan to peepe,
Depriu'd so soone of my sweet Dreame, gan almost weepe.

The Conclusion.

Thus, sacred Virgin, Muse of chastitie,
  This difference is betwixt the Moone and thee:
  Shee shines by Night; but thou by Day do'st shine:
Shee Monthly changeth; thou dost nere decline:
And as the Sunne, to her, doth lend his light,
So hee, by thee, is onely made so bright:
Yet neither Sun, nor Moone, thou canst be named,
Because thy light hath both their beauties shamed:
  Then, since an heauenly Name doth thee befall,
  Thou V I R G O art: (if any Signe at all).

FINIS.

[SONNETS.]

SONNET. I.

Sporting at fancie, setting light by loue,
   There came a theefe, and stole away my heart,
   (And therefore robd me of my chiefest part)
Yet cannot Reason him a felon proue.
For why his beauty (my hearts thiefe) affirmeth,
Piercing no skin (the bodies fensiue wall)
And hauing leaue, and free consent withall,
Himselfe not guilty, from loue guilty tearmeth,
Conscience the Iudge, twelue Reasons are the Iurie,
   They finde mine eies the be[a]utie t' haue let in,
   And on this verdict giuen, agreed they bin,
VVherefore, because his beauty did allure yee,
   Your Doome is this: in teares still to be drowned,
   VVhen his faire forehead with disdain is frowned.

SONNET. II.

B[a]uty and Maiesty are falne at ods,
   Th'one claimes his cheeke, the other claimes
      his chin;
   Then Vertue comes, and puts her title in.
(Quoth she) I make him like th'immortall Gods.
(Quoth Maiestie) I owne his lookes, his Brow,
   His lips, (quoth Loue) his eies, his faire is mine.
   And yet (quoth Maiesty) he is not thine,
I mixe Disdaine with Loues congealed Snow.
I, but (quoth Loue) his lockes are mine (by right)
   His stately gate is mine (quoth Maiestie,)
   And mine (quoth Vertue) is his Modestie.
Thus as they striue about this heauenly wight,
   At last the other two to Vertue yeeld,
   The lists of Loue, fought in faire Beauties field.

SONNET. III.

The Stoicks thinke, (and they come neere the truth,)
   That vertue is the chiefest good of all,
   The Academicks on *Idea* call.
   The Epicures in pleasure spend their youth,
The Perrepatetickes iudge felicitie,
   To be the chiefest good aboue all other,
   One man, thinks this: and that conceaues another:
So that in one thing very few agree.
Let Stoicks haue their Vertue if they will,
   And all the rest their chiefe-supposed good,
   Let cruell Martialists delight in blood,
And Mysers ioy their bags with gold to fill:
   My chiefest good, my chiefe felicity,
   Is to be gazing on my loues faire eie.

SONNET. IIII.

Two stars there are in one faire firmament,
   (Of some intitled *Ganymedes* sweet face),
   VVhich other stars in brightnes doe disgrace,
As much as *Po* in clearenes passeth *Trent*.
Nor are they common natur'd stars: for why,
   These stars when other shine vaile their pure light,
   And when all other vanish out of sight,
They adde a glory to the worlds great eie.
By these two stars my life is onely led,
   In them I place my ioy, in them my pleasure,
   Loue's piercing Darts, and Natures precious treasure
With their sweet foode my fainting soule is fed:
   Then when my sunne is absent from my sight
   How can it chuse (with me) but be dark night?

SONNET. V.

It is reported of faire *Thetis* Sonne,
   (*Achilles* famous for his chiualry,
   His noble minde and magnanimity,)
That when the Troian wars were new begun,
Whos'euer was deepe-wounded with his speare,
   Could neuer be recured of his maime,
   Nor euer after be made whole againe:
Except with that speares rust he holpen were.
Euen so it fareth with my fortune now,
   Who being wounded with his piercing eie,
   Must either thereby finde a remedy,
Or els to be releeu'd, I know not how.
   Then if thou hast a minde still to annoy me,
   Kill me with kisses, if thou wilt destroy me.

SONNET. VI.

SWeet Corrall lips, where Nature's treasure lies,
    The balme of blisse, the soueraigne salue of sorrow,
    The secret touch of loues heart-burning arrow,
Come quench my thirst or els poor *Daphnis* dies.
One night I dream'd (alas twas but a Dreame)
    That I did feele the sweetnes of the same,
    Where-with inspir'd, I young againe became,
And from my heart a spring of blood did streame,
But when I wak't, I found it nothing so,
    Saue that my limbs (me thought) did waxe more strong
    And I more lusty far, and far more yong.
This gift on him rich Nature did bestow.
    Then if in dreaming so, I so did speede,
    What should I doe, if I did so indeede?

SONNET. VII.

SWeet *Thames* I honour thee, not for thou art
    The chiefest Riuer of the fairest Ile,
    Nor for thou dost admirers eies beguile,
But for thou hold'st the keeper of my heart,
For on thy waues, (thy Christal-billow'd waues,)
    My fairest faire, my siluer Swan is swimming:
    Against the sunne his pruned feathers trimming:
Whilst *Neptune* his faire feete with water laues,
Neptune, I feare not thee, not yet thine eie,
    And yet (alas) *Apollo* lou'd a boy,
    And *Cyparissus* was *Siluanus* ioy.
No, no, I feare none but faire *Thetis*, I,
    For if she spie my Loue, (alas) aie me,
    My mirth is turn'd to extreame miserie.

SONNET. VIII.

Ometimes I wish that I his pillow were,
   So might I steale a kisse, and yet not seene,
   So might I gaze vpon his sleeping eine,
Although I did it with a panting feare:
But when I well consider how vaine my wish is,
   Ah foolish Bees (thinke I) that doe not sucke
   His lips for hony; but poore flowers doe plucke
Which haue no sweet in them: when his sole kisses,
Are able to reuiue a dying soule.
   Kisse him, but sting him not, for if you doe,
   His angry voice your flying will pursue:
But when they heare his tongue, what can controule,
   Their back-returne? for then they plaine may see,
   How hony-combs from his lips dropping bee.

SONNET. IX.

Iana (on a time) walking the wood,
   To sport herselfe, of her faire traine forlorne,
   Chaunc't for to pricke her foote against a thorne,
And from thence issu'd out a streame of blood.
No sooner shee was vanisht out of sight,
   But loues faire Queen came there away by chance,
   And hauing of this hap a glym'ring glance,
She put the blood into a christall bright,
When being now come vnto mount *Rhodope*,
   With her faire hands she formes a shape of Snow,
   And blends it with this blood; from whence doth grow
A louely creature, brighter than the Dey.
   And being christned in faire *Paphos* shrine,
   She call'd him *Ganymede*: as all diuine.

SONNET. X.

Thus was my loue, thus was my *Ganymed*,
    (Heauens ioy, worlds wonder, natures fairest
        work,
In whose aspect Hope and Dispaire doe lurke)
Made of pure blood in whitest snow yshed,
And for sweete *Venus* only form'd his face,
    And his each member delicately framed,
    And last of all faire *Ganymede* him named,
His limbs (as their Creatrix) her imbrace.
But as for his pure, spotles, vertuous minde,
    Because it sprung of chaste *Dianaes* blood,
    (Goddesse of Maides, directresse of all good,)
Hit wholy is to chastity inclinde.
    And thus it is: as far as I can proue,
    He loues to be beloued, but not to loue.

SONNET XI.

Sighing, and sadly sitting by my Loue,
    He ask't the cause of my hearts sorrowing,
    Coniuring me by heauens eternall King
To tell the cause which me so much did moue.
Compell'd: (quoth I) to thee will I confesse,
    Loue is the cause; and only loue it is
    That doth depriue me of my heauenly blisse.
Loue is the paine that doth my heart oppresse.
And what is she (quoth he) whom thou dos't loue?
    Looke in this glasse (quoth I) there shalt thou see
    The perfect forme of my fælicitie.
When, thinking that it would strange Magique proue,
    He open'd it: and taking of the couer,
    He straight perceau'd himselfe to be my Louer.

SONNET. XII.

Some talke of *Ganymede* th' *Idalian* Boy,
    And some of faire *Adonis* make their boast,
    Some talke of him whom louely *Læda* lost,
And some of *Ecchoes* loue that was so coy.
They speake by heere-say, I of perfect truth,
    They partially commend the persons named,
    And for them, sweet Encomions haue framed:
I onely t'him haue sacrifized my youth.
As for those wonders of antiquitie,
    And those whom later ages haue inioy'd,
    (But ah what hath not cruell death destroide?
Death, that enuies this worlds felicitie),
    They were (perhaps) lesse faire then Poets write.
    But he is fairer then I can indite.

SONNET. XIII.

Speake Eccho, tell; how may I call my loue? *Loue.*
    But how his Lamps that are so christa-
        line? *Eyne.*
    Oh happy starrs that make your heauens diuine:
And happy Iems that admiration moue.
How tearm'st his golden tresses wau'd with aire? *Haire.*
    Oh louely haire of your more-louely Maister,
    Image of loue, faire shape of Alablaster,
Why do'st thou driue thy Louer to dispaire?
How do'st thou cal the bed wher beuty grows? *Rose.*
    Faire virgine-Rose, whose mayden blossoms couer
    The milke-white Lilly, thy imbracing Louer:
Whose kisses makes thee oft thy red to lose.
    And blushing oft for shame, when he hath kist thee,
    He vades away, and thou raing'st where it list thee.

SONNET. XIIII.

Ere, hold this gloue (this milk-white cheueril gloue)
    Not quaintly ouer-wrought with curious knots,
    Not deckt with golden spangs, nor siluer spots,
Yet wholsome for thy hand as thou shalt proue.
Ah no; (sweet boy) place this gloue neere thy heart,
    Weare it, and lodge it still within thy brest,
    So shalt thou make me (most vnhappy,) blest.
So shalt thou rid my paine, and ease my smart:
How can that be (perhaps) thou wilt reply,
    A gloue is for the hand not for the heart,
    Nor can it well be prou'd by common art,
Nor reasons rule. To this, thus answere I:
    If thou from gloue do'st take away the g,
    Then gloue is loue: and so I send it thee.

SONNET. XV.

[H] fairest *Ganymede*, disdaine me not,
    Though silly Sheepeheard I, presume to loue thee,
    Though my harsh songs and Sonnets cannot moue thee,
Yet to thy beauty is my loue no blot.
Apollo, Ioue, and many Gods beside,
    S' daind not the name of cuntry shepheards swains,
    Nor want we pleasure, though we take some pains,
We liue contentedly: a thing call'd pride,
Which so corrupts the Court and euery place,
    (Each place I meane where learning is neglected,
    And yet of late, euen learnings selfe's infected)
I know not what it meanes, in any case:
    Wee onely (when *Molorchus* gins to peepe)
    Learne for to folde, and to vnfold our sheepe.

SONNET. XVI.

Ong haue I long'd to see my Loue againe,
    Still haue I wisht, but neuer could obtaine it;
    Rather than all the world (if I might gaine it)
Would I desire my loues sweet precious gaine.
Yet in my soule I see him euerie day,
    See him, and see his still sterne countenaunce,
    But (ah) what is of long continuance,
Where Maiestie and Beautie beares the sway?
Sometimes, when I imagine that I see him,
    (As loue is full of foolish fantasies)
    VVeening to kisse his lips, as my loues fee's,
I feele but Aire: nothing but Aire to bee him.
    Thus with *Ixion*, kisse I clouds in vaine:
    Thus with *Ixion*, feele I endles paine.

SONNET. XVII.

Herry-lipt *Adonis* in his snowie shape,
    Might not compare with his pure Iuorie white,
    On whose faire front a Poets pen may write,
Whose rosiate red excels the crimson grape,
His loue-enticing delicate soft limbs,
    Are rarely fram'd t'intrap poore gazing eies:
    His cheekes, the Lillie and Carnation dies,
With louely tincture which *Apolloes* dims.
His lips ripe strawberries in Nectar wet,
    His mouth a Hiue, his tongue a hony-combe,
    Where Muses (like Bees) make their mansion.
His teeth pure Pearle in blushing Correll set.
    Oh how can such a body sinne-procuring,
    Be slow to loue, and quicke to hate, enduring?

SONNET. XVIII.

Ot *Megabætes* nor *Cleonymus*,
 (Of whom great *Plutarch* makes such mention,
 Praysing their faire with rare inuention)
As *Ganymede* were halfe so beauteous.
They onely pleas'd the eies of two great Kings,
 But all the worlde at my loue stands amazed,
 Nor one that on his Angels face hath gazed,
But (rauisht with delight) him Presents brings.
Some weaning Lambs, and some a suckling Kyd,
 Some Nuts, and fil-beards, others Peares and Plums,
 Another with a milk-white Heyfar comes;
As lately *Ægons* man (*Damætas*) did:
 But neither he, nor all the Nymphs beside,
 Can win my *Ganymede*, with them t'abide.

SONNET. XIX.

H no; nor I my selfe: though my pure loue
 (Sweete *Ganymede*) to thee hath still beene pure,
 And euen till my last gaspe shall aie endure,
Could euer thy obdurate beuty moue:
Then cease oh Goddesse sonne (for sure thou art,
 A Goddesse sonne that canst resist desire)
 Cease thy hard heart, and entertaine loues fire,
Within thy sacred breast: by Natures art.
And as I loue thee more then any Creature,
 (Loue thee, because thy beautie is diuine;
 Loue thee, because my selfe, my soule is thine:
Wholie deuoted to thy louelie feature),
 Euen so of all the vowels, I and V,
 Are dearest vnto me, as doth ensue.

SONNET. XX.

But now my Muse toyld with continuall care,
   Begins to faint, and slacke her former pace,
   Expecting fauour from that heauenly grace,
That maie (in time) her feeble strength repaire.
Till when (sweete youth) th'essence of my soule,
   (Thou that dost sit and sing at my hearts griefe.
   Thou that dost send thy shepheard no reliefe)
Beholde, these lines; the sonnes of Teares and Dole.
Ah had great *Colin* chiefe of sheepheards all,
   Or gentle *Rowland*, my professed friend,
   Had they thy beautie, or my pennance pend,
Greater had beene thy fame, and lesse my fall:
   But since that euerie one cannot be wittie,
   Pardon I craue of them, and of thee, pitty.

FINIS.

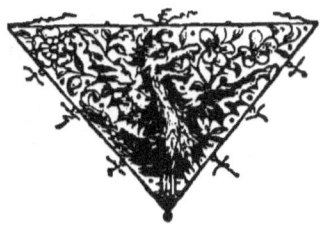

AN ODE.

Ights were short, and daies were long;
Blossoms on the Hauthorn's hung:
Philomæle (Night-Musiques-King)
Tolde the comming of the spring.
Whose sweete siluer-sounding voice
Made the little birds reioice:
Skipping light from spray to spray,
Till *Aurora* shew'd the day.
Scarce might one see, when I might see
(For such chaunces sudden bee)
By a well of Marble-stone
A Shepheard lying all alone.
Weepe he did; and his weeping
Made the fading flowers spring.
Daphnis was his name (I weene)
Youngest Swaine of Summers Queene.
When *Aurora* saw 'twas he.
Weepe she did for companie:
Weepe she did for her sweete sonne
That (when antique *Troy* was wonne)
Suffer'd death by lucklesse fate,
Whom she now laments too late:
And each morning (by Cocks crew)
Showers downe her siluer dew.
Whose teares (falling from their spring)
Giue moysture to each liuing thing,
That on earth increase and grow,

AN ODE.

Through power of their friendlie foe.
Whose effect when *Flora* felt,
Teares, that did her bosome melt,
(For who can resist teares often,
But Shee whom no teares can soften?)
Peering straite aboue the banks,
Shew'd herselfe to giue her thanks.
Wondring thus at Natures worke,
(Wherein many maruailes lurke)
Me thought I heard a dolefull noise,
Consorted with a mournfull voice,
Drawing nie to heare more plaine,
Heare I did, vnto my paine,
(For who is not pain'd to heare
Him in griefe whom heart holdes deare?)
Silly swaine (with griefe ore-gone)
Thus to make his piteous mone.
Loue I did, (alas the while)
Loue I did, but did beguile
My deare loue with louing so,
(VVhom as then I did not know.)
Loue I did the fairest boy,
That these fields did ere enioy.
Loue I did, fair *Ganymed*;
(*Venus* darling, beauties bed:)
Him I thought the fairest creature;
Him the quintessence of Nature:
But yet (alas) I was deceiu'd,
(Loue of reason is bereau'd)
For since then I saw a Lasse.
(Lasse) that did in beauty passe,
(Passe) faire *Ganymede* as farre
As *Phœbus* doth the smallest starre.
Loue commaunded me to loue;
Fancy bade me not remoue
My affection from the swaine

AN ODE.

Which he cannot graunt the crauer?)
Loue at last (though loath) preuailde;
(Loue) that so my heart assailde;
Whom I neuer could obtaine:
(For who can obtaine that fauour,
Wounding me with her faire eies,
(Ah how Loue can subtelize,
And deuize a thousand shifts,
How to worke men to his drifts.)
Her it is, for whom I mourne;
Her, for whom my life I scorne;
Her, for whom I weepe all day;
Her, for whom I sigh, and say,
Either She, or els no creature,
Shall enioy my loue: whose feature
Though I neuer can obtaine,
Yet shall my true loue remaine:
Till (my body turn'd to clay)
My poore soule must passe away,
To the heauens; where (I hope)
Hit shall finde a resting scope:
Then since I loued thee (alone)
Remember me when I am gone.
Scarce had he these last words spoken,
But me thought his heart was broken;
With great griefe that did abound,
(Cares and griefe the heart confound)
In whose heart (thus riu'd in three)
ELIZA written I might see:
In Caracters of crimson blood,
(VVhose meaning well I vnderstood.)
Which, for my heart might not behold,
I hyed me home my sheep to folde.

FINIS.

CASSANDRA.

Pon a gorgious gold embossed bed,   [sunne,
With Tissue curtaines drawne against the
(Which gazers eies into amazement led,
So curiously the workmanship was done,)
   Lay faire *Cassandra,*in her snowie smocke,
   Whose lips the Rubies and the pearles did locke.

And from her Iuory front hung dangling downe,
A bush of long and louely curled haire;
VVhose head impalled with a precious Crowne
Of orient Pearle, made her to seeme more faire:
   And yet more faire she hardly could be thought,
   Then Loue and Nature in her face had wrought.

By this, young *Phœbus* rising from the East,
Had tane a view of this rare Paragon:
Wherewith he soone his radiant beames addresst,
And with great ioy her (sleeping) gazed vpon:
   Til at the last, through her light cazements cleare,
   He stole a kisse; and softly call'd her Deare.

Yet not so softly but (therwith awak't,)
Shee gins to open her faire christall couers,
Wherewith the wounded God, for terror quakt,
(Viewing those darts that kill disdained louers:)
   And blushing red to see himselfe so shamed
   He scorns his Coach, and his owne beauty blamed.

Now with a trice he leaues the azure skies,
(As whilome *Ioue* did at *Europaes* rape,)
And rauisht with her loue-a[l]luring eies,
He turns himselfe into a humane shape:
    And that his wish the sooner might ensue,
    He sutes himselfe like one of *Venus* crew.

Vpon his head he wore a Hunters hat
Of crimson veluet, spangd with stars of gold,
Which grac'd his louely face: and ouer that
A siluer hatband ritchly to behold:
    On his left shoulder hung a loose *Tyara*,
    As whilome vs'd faire *Penthesilea*.

Faire *Penthesilea* th'*Amazonian* Queene,
When she to Troy came with her warlike band,
Of braue Viragoes glorious to be seene;
Whose manlike force no power might withstand:
    So look't *Apollo* in his louely weedes,
    As he vnto the Troian Damzell speedes.

Not faire, *Adonis* in his chiefest pride,
Did seeme more faire, then young *Apollo* seemed,
When he through th'aire inuisibly did glide,
T'obtaine his Loue, which he Angelike deemed;
    Whom finding in her chamber all alone,
    He thus begins t'expresse his piteous mone.

O fairest, faire, aboue all faires (quoth hee)
If euer Loue obtained Ladies fauour,
Then shew thy selfe compassionate to me,
Whose head surpriz'd with thy diuine behauior,
    Yeelds my selfe captiue to thy conqu'ring eies:
    O then shew mercy, do not tyrannize.

Scarce had *Apollo* vtter'd these last words
(Rayning downe pearle from his immortall eies)
When she for answere, naught but feare affords,
Filling the place with lamentable cries:
    But *Phœbus* fearing much these raging fits,
    With sugred kisses sweetely charm'd her lips.

(And tells her softly in her softer eare)
That he a God is, and no mortall creature:
Wherewith abandoning all needlesse feare,
(A common frailtie of weake womans nature)
   She boldly askes him of his deitie,
   Gracing her question with her wanton eie.

Which charge to him no sooner was assignde,
But taking faire *Cassandra* by the hand
(The true bewraier of his secrete minde)
He first begins to let her vnderstand,
   That he from *Demogorgon* was descended:
   Father of th'Earth, of Gods and men commended.

The tenor of which tale he now recites,
Closing each period with a rauisht kisse:
Which kindnes, she vnwillingly requites,
Conioyning oft her Corrall lips to his:
   Not that she lou'd the loue of any one;
   But that she meant to cozen him anone.

Hee briefly t'her relates his pedegree:
The sonne of *Ioue*, sole guider of the sunne,
He that slue *Python* so victoriouslie,
He that the name of wisdomes God hath wonne,
   The God of Musique, and of Poetry:
   Of Phisicke, Learning, and Chirurgery.

All which he eloquently reckons vp,
That she might know how great a God he was:
And being charm'd with *Cupid's* golden cup
He partiallie vnto her praise doth passe,
   Calling her tipe of honour, Queen of beauty:
   To whom all eies owe tributary duety.

I loued once, (quoth hee) aie me I lou'd,
As faire a shape as euer nature framed:
Had she not been so hard t'haue beene remou'd,
By birth a sea-Nymph; cruell *Daphne* named:
   Whom, for shee would not to my will agree,
   The Gods transform'd into a Laurell tree.

Ah therefore be not, (with that word he kist her)
Be not (quot[h] he) so proud as *Daphne* was:
Ne care thou for the anger of my sister,
She cannot, nay she shall not hurt my *Cass*:
   For if she doe, I vow (by dreadfull night)
   Neuer againe to lend her of my light.

This said: he sweetly doth imbrace his loue,
Yoaking his armes about her Iuory necke:
And calls her wanton *Venus* milk-white Doue,
VVhose ruddie lips the damaske roses decke.
   And euer as his tongue compiles her praise,
   Loue daintie Dimples in her cheekes doth raise.

And meaning now to worke her stratagem
Vpon the silly God, that thinks none ill,
She hugs him in her armes, and kisses him;
(Th'easlyer to intice him to her will.)
   And being not able to maintaine the feeld,
   Thus she begins (or rather seemes) to yeeld.

VVoon with thy words, and rauisht with my beauty,
Loe here *Cassandra* yeelds her selfe to thee,
Requiring nothing for thy vowed duety,
But only firmnesse, Loue, and secrecy:
   Which for that now (euen now) I meane to try thee,
   A boone I craue; which thou canst not deny me.

Scarce were these honywords breath'd from her lips,
But he, supposing that she ment good-faith,
Her filed tongues temptations interceps;
And (like a Nouice,) thus to her he saith:
   Aske what thou wilt, and I will giue it thee;
   Health, wealth, long life, wit, art, or dignitie.

Here-with she blushing red, (for shame did adde
A crimson tincture to her palish hew,)
Seeming in outward semblance passing glad,
(As one that th'end of her petition knew)
   She makes him sweare by vgly *Acheron*,
   That he his promise should performe anon.

Which done : relying on his sacred oath,
She askes of him the gift of prophecie :
He (silent) giues consent : though seeming loath
To grant so much to fraile mortalitie :
  But since that he his vowes maie not recall,
  He giues to her the sp'rite propheticall.

But she no sooner had obtain'd her wish,
VVhen straite vnpris'ning her lasciuiuous armes
From his softe bosom (th'aluary of blisse)
She chastely counterchecks loues hote alarmes :
  And fearing lest his presence might offend her,
  She slips aside ; and (absent) doth defend her.

    (*Muliere ne credas, ne mortuæ quidem.*)

Looke how a brightsome Planet in the skie,
(Spangling the Welkin with a golden spot)
Shootes suddenly from the beholders eie,
And leaues him looking there where she is not :
  Euen so amazed *Phœbus* (to descrie her)
  Lookes all about, but no where can espie her.

Not th'hungry Lyon, hauing lost his pray,
With greater furie runneth through the wood,
(Making no signe of momentarie staie,
Till he haue satisfi'd himslfe with blood,)
  Then angry *Phœbus* mounts into the skie :
  Threatning the world with his hot-burning eie.

Now nimbly to his glist'ring Coach he skips,
And churlishlie ascends his loftie chaire,
Yerking his head strong Iades with yron whips,
Whose fearefull neighing ecchoes through the aire,
  Snorting out fierie Sulphure from theire nosethrils :
  Whose deadly damp the worlds poore people kils.

Him leaue me (for a while) amids the heauens,
VVreaking his anger on his sturdie steedes :
Whose speedfull course the day and night now eeuens,
(The earth dis-robed of her summer weedes)
  And nowe black-mantled night with her browne vaile,
  Couers each thing that all the world might quaile.

VVhen loe, *Cassandra* lying at her rest,
(Her rest were restlesse thoughts:) it so befell,
Her minde with multitude of cares opprest,
Requir'd some sleepe her passions to expell:
    VVhich when sad *Morpheus* will did vnderstand,
    He clos'd her eie-lids with his leaden hand.

Now sleepeth shee: and as shee sleepes, beholde;
Shee seemes to see the God whom late shee wronged
Standing before her; whose fierce looks vnfold,
His hidden wrath (to whom iust ire belonged)
    Seeing, shee sighs, and sighing quak't for feare,
    To see the shaddow of her shame appeare.

Betwixt amaze and dread as shee thus stands,
The fearefull vision drew more neere vnto her:
Aud pynioning her armes in captiue bands
So sure, that mortall wight may not vndoe her,
    He with a bloudy knife (oh cruell part,)
    VVith raging fury stabd her to the heart.

Heerewith awaking from her slumbring sleepe,
(For feare, and care, are enemies to rest:)
At such time as *Aurora* gins to peepe
And shew her selfe; far orient in the East:
    Shee heard a voice which said: O wicked woman,
    Why dost thou stil the gods to vengeance summon?

Thou shalt (indeede) fore-tell of things to come;
And truely, too; (for why my vowes are past)
But heare the end of *Ioues* eternall doome:
Because thy promise did so little last,
    Although thou tell the truth, (this gift I giue thee)
    Yet for thy falsehood, no man shall beleeue thee.

And (for thy sake) this pennance I impose
Vpon the remnant of all woman kinde,
For that they be such truth professed foes;
A constant woman shall be hard to finde:
    And that all flesh at my dread name may tremble,
    When they weep most, then shall they most dissemble.

This said *Apollo* then: And since that time
His words haue proved true as Oracles:
Whose turning thoughtes ambitiously doe clime
To heauens height; and world with lightnes fils:
    VVhose sex are subject to inconstancie,
    As other creatures are to destinie.

Yet famous *Sabrine* on thy banks doth rest
The fairest Maide that euer world admired:
Whose constant minde, with heauenly gifts possest
Makes her rare selfe of all the world desired.
    In whose chaste thoughts no vanitie doth enter;
    So pure a minde *Endymions* Love hath lent her.

Queene of my thoughts, but subiect of my verse,
(Divine *Eliza*) pardon my defect:
Whose artlesse pen so rudely doth reherse
Thy beauties worth; (for want of due respect)
    Oh pardon thou the follies of my youth;
    Pardon my faith, my loue, my zeale, my truth.

But to *Cassandra* now: who hauing heard
The cruell sentence of the threatning voice;
At length (too late) begins to waxe affeard,
Lamenting much her vnrepentant choice:
    And seeing her hard hap without reliefe,
    She sheeds salt teares in token of her griefe.

VVhich when *Aurora* saw, and saw t'was shee,
Euen shee her selfe whose far-renowmed fame
Made all the world to wonder at her beauty,
It mou'd compassion in this ruthfull Dame:
    And thinking on her Sonnes sad destinie,
    With mournfull teares she beares her companie.

Great was the mone, which faire *Cassandra* made:
Greater the kindnesse, which *Aurora* shew'd:
VVhose sorrow with the sunne began to fade,
And her moist teares on th'earths green grasse bestow'd:
    Kissing the flowers with her siluer dew,
    VVhose fading beautie, seem'd her case to rew.

Scarce was the louely Easterne Queene departed,
From stately *Ilion* (whose proud-reared wals
Seem'd to controule the cloudes, till *Vulcan* darted
Against their Tower his burning fier-bals)
   When sweet *Cassandra* (leauing her soft bed)
   In seemely sort her selfe apparelled.

And hearing that her honourable Sire,
(Old princely *Pryamus Troy*'s aged King)
Was gone into *Ioues* Temple, to conspire
Against the *Greekes*, (whom he to war did bring)
   Shee, (like a Furie), in a bedlam rage,
   Runs gadding thither, his fell wrath t'assuage.

But not preuailing: truely she fore-tolde
The fall of *Troy* (with bold erected face:)
They count her hare-brain'd, mad, and ouer-bold,
To presse in presence in so graue a place:
   But in meane season *Paris* he is gone,
   To bring destruction on faire *Ilion*.

What, ten-yeeres siedge by force could not subuert,
That, two false traitors in one night destroi'd:
Who richly guerdon'd for their bad desert,
VVas of *Æneas* but small time inioi'd:
   VVho, for concealement of *Achilles* loue,
   VVas banished; from *Ilion* to remoue.

King *Pryam* dead and all the Troians slaine;
(His sonnes, his friends and deere confederates)
And lots now cast for captiues that remaine,
(Whom Death hath spared for more cruell fates)
   Cassandra then to *Agamemnon* fell,
   With whom a Lemman she disdain'd to dwell.

She, weepes; he, wooes; he would, but she would not:
He, tell's his birth; shee, pleades virginitie:
He saith, selfe-pride doth rarest beauty blot:
(And with that word he kist her louingly:)
   Shee, yeeldingly resists; he faines to die:
   Shee, fall's for feare; he, on her feareleslie.

But this braue generall of all the *Greekes*,
VVas quickly foyled at a womans hands,
For who so rashly such incounters seekes,
Of hard mis-hap in danger euer stands:
   Onely chaste thoughts, vertuous abstinence,
   Gainst such sweet poyson is the sur'st defence.

But who can shun the force of beauties blow?
Who is not rauisht with a louely looke?
Grac'd with a wanton eie, (the hearts dumb show)
Such fish are taken with a siluer hooke:
   And when true loue cannot these pearles obtaine
   Vnguentum Album is the only meane.

Farre be it from my thought (diuinest Maid)
To haue relation to thy heauenly hew,
(In whose sweete voice the Muses are imbaid)
No pen can paint thy commendation due:
   Saue only that pen, which no pen can be,
   An Angels quill, to make a pen for thee.

But to returne to these vnhappie Louers,
(Sleeping securely in each others armes)
VVhose sugred ioies nights sable mantle couers,
Little regarding their ensuing harmes:
   VVhich afterward they iointlie both repented:
   " Fate is fore-seene, but neuer is preuented."

Which saying to be true, this lucklesse Dame
Approued in the sequele of her story:
Now waxing pale, now blushing red (for shame),
She seales her lips with silence (womens glory)
   Till *Agamemnon* vrging her replies,
   Thus of his death she truely prophecies.

The day shall come, (quoth she) O dismal daie!
When thou by false *Ægistus* shalt be slaine:
Heere could she tell no more; but made a stay.
(From further speech as willing to refraine :)
   Not knowing then, nor little did she thinke,
   That she with him of that same cup must drinke

But what? (fond man) he laughs her skil to scorne,
And iesteth at her diuination:
Ah to what vnbeliefe are Princes borne?
(The onely ouer-throw of many a Nation:)
   And so it did befall this lucklesse Prince,
   Whom all the world hath much lamented since.

Insteede of teares, he smileth at her tale:
Insteede of griefe, he makes great shew of gladnes:
But after blisse, there euer followes bale;
And after mirth, there alwaies commeth sadnes:
   But gladnesse, blisse, and mirth had so possest him,
   That sadnes, bale, and griefe could not molest him.

Oh cruell *Parcæ* (quoth *Cassandra* then)
Why are you *Parcæ*, yet not mou'd with praier?
Oh small security of mortall men,
That liue on earth, and breathe this vitall aire:
   When we laugh most, then are we next to sorrow;
   The Birds feede vs to-day, we them to-morrow.

But if the first did little moue his minde,
Her later speeches lesse with him preuailed;
Who beinge wholy to selfe-will inclinde,
Deemes her weake braine with lunacy assailed:
   And still the more shee councels him to stay,
   The more he striueth to make haste away.

How on the Seas he scap'd stormes, rocks and sholes,
(Seas that enuide the conquest he had wone,
Gaping like hell to swallow Greekish soules,)
I heere omit; onely suppose it done:
   His storm-tyrde Barke safely brings him to shore,
   His whole Fleete els, or suncke or lost before.

Lift vp thy head, thou ashie-cyndred *Troy*,
See the commaunder of thy traitor foes,
That made thy last nights woe, his first daies ioie,
Now gins his night of ioy and daie of woes:
   His fall be thy delight, thine was his pride:
   As he thee then, so now thou him deride.

He and *Cassandra* now are set on shore,
VVhich he salutes with ioy, she greetes with teares,
Currors are sent that poast to Court before,
Whose tidings fill th'adultrous Queene with feares,
   Who with *Ægistus* in a lust-staind bed,
   Her selfe, her King, her State dishonored.

She wakes the lecher with a loud-strain'd shrike,
Loue-toies they leaue, now doth lament begin:
Ile flie (quoth he) but she doth that mislike,
Guilt vnto guilt, and sinne she ads to sinne:
   Shee meanes to kill (immodest loue to couer)
   A kingly husband, for a caytiue louer.

The peoples ioies, conceiued at his returne,
Their thronging multitudes: their gladsome cries,
Their gleeful hymnes, whiles piles of incense burne:
Their publique shewes, kept at solemnities:
   We passe: and tell how King and Queene did meet,
   Where he with zeale, she him with guile did greet.

He (noble Lord) fearelesse of hidden treason,
Sweetely salutes this weeping Crocodile:
Excusing euery cause with instant reason
That kept him from her sight so long a while:
   She, faintly pardons him; smiling by Art:
   (For life was in her lookes, death in her hart.)

For pledge that I am pleas'd receiue (quoth shee)
This rich wrought robe, thy *Clytemnestras* toile:
Her ten yeeres worke this day shall honour thee,
For ten yeeres war, and one daies glorious spoile:
   Whil'st thou contendedst there, I heere did this:
   Weare it my loue, my life, my ioy, my blisse.

Scarce had the Syren said what I haue write,
But he (kind Prince) by her milde words misled,
Receiu'd the robe, to trie if it were fit;
(The robe) that had no issue for his head;
   Which, whilst he vainly hoped to haue found,
   Ægistus pierst him with a mortal wound.

Oh how the *Troyan* Damzell was amazed
To see so fell and bloudy a Tragedie,
Performed in one Act; she naught but gazed,
Vpon the picture; whom shee dead did see,
  Before her face: whose body she emballms,
  With brennish teares, and sudden deadly qualms.

Faine would she haue fled backe on her swift horse
But *Clytemnestra* bad her be content,
Her time was com'n: now bootelesse vsd she force,
Against so many; whom this Tygresse sent
  To apprehend her: who (within one hower
  Brought backe againe) was lockt within a Tower.

Now is she ioylesse, friendlesse, and (in fine)
Without all hope of further libertie:
Insteed of cates, cold water was her wine,
And *Agamemnons* corps her meate must be,
  Or els she must for hunger starue (poore sole)
  What could she do but make great mone and dole.

So darke the dungeon was, wherein she was,
That neither Sunne (by day) nor Mone (by night)
Did shew themselues: and thus it came to passe.
The Sunne denide to lend his glorious light
  To such a periur'd wight, or to be seene;
  (What neede she light, that ouer-light had bin?)

Now silent night drew on; when all things sleepe,
Saue theeues, and cares; and now stil mid-night came:
When sad *Cassandra* did naught els but weepe;
Oft calling on her *Agamemnons* name.
  But seeing that the dead did not replie,
  Thus she begins to mourne, lament, and crie.

Oh cruell Fortune (mother of despaire,)
Well art thou christen'd with a cruell name:
Since thou regardest not the wise, or faire,
But do'st bestow thy riches (to thy shame)
  On fooles and lowly swaines, that care not for thee:
  And yet I weepe, and yet thou do'st abhorre me.

Fie on ambition, fie on filthy pride,
The roote of ill, the cause of all my woe:
On whose fraile yce my youth first slipt aside:
And falling downe, receiu'd a fatall blow.
   Ah who hath liu'd to see such miserie
   As I haue done, and yet I cannot die?

I liu'd (quoth she) to see *Troy* set on fire:
I liu'd to see, renowned *Hector* slaine:
I liu'd to see, the shame of my desire:
And yet I liue, to feel my grieuous paine:
   Let all young maides example take by me,
   To keepe their oathes, and spotlesse chastity.

Happy are they, that neuer liu'd to know
What 'tis to liue in this world happily:
Happy are they which neuer yet felt woe:
Happy are they, that die in infancie:
   Whose sins are cancell'd in their mothers wombe:
   Whose cradle is their graue, whose lap their tomb.

Here ended shee; and then her teares began,
That (Chorus-like) at euery word downe rained.
VVhich like a paire of christall fountaines ran,
Along her louely cheekes: with roses stained:
   Which as they wither still (for want of raine)
   Those siluer showers water them againe.

Now had the poore-mans clock (shrill chauntcleare)
Twice giuen notice of the Mornes approach,
(That then began in glorie to appeare,
Drawne in her stately colour'd saffron-Coach)
   VVhen shee (poore Lady) almost turn'd to teares,
   Began to teare and rend her golden haires.

Lie there (quoth shee) the workers of my woes
You trifling toies, which my liues staine haue bin:
You, by whose meanes our coines chiefly growes,
Clothing the backe with pride, the soule with sin:
   Lie there (quoth shee) the causers of my care;
   This said, her robes she all in pieces tare.

Here-with, as weary of her wretched life,
(VVhich shee inioy'd with small felicitie)
She ends her fortune with a fatall knife;
(First day of ioy, last day of miserie:)
   Then why is death accounted Nature's foe,
   Since death (indeed) is but the end of woe?

For as by death, her bodie was released
From that strong prison made of lime and stone;
Euen so by death her purest soule was eased,
From bodies prison, and from endlesse mone:
   VVhere now shee walkes in sweete *Elysium*
   (The place for wrongful Death and Martirdum.)

FINIS.

The Encomion of Lady Pecunia:
OR
The praife of Money.

*quærenda pecunia primum est,
Virtus post nummos.*   Horace.

By *Richard Barnfeild*, Graduate in *Oxford*.

LONDON,
Printed by G. S. for Iohn Iaggard, and are
to be sold at his shoppe neere Temple-barre,
at the Signe of the Hand and starre.
1598.

To the Gentlemen Readers.

Entlemen, being incouraged through your gentle acceptance of my *Cynthia*, I haue once more aduentured on your Curtesies: hoping to finde you (as I haue done heretofore) friendly. Being determined to write of somthing, and yet not resolued of any thing, I considered with my selfe, if one should write of Loue (they will say) why, euery one writes of Loue: if of Vertue, why, who regards Vertue? To be short, I could thinke of nothing, but either it was common, or not at all in request. At length I bethought my selfe of a Subiect, both new (as hauing neuer beene written vpon before) and pleasing (as I thought) because Mans Nature (commonly) loues to heare that praised, with whose pressence, hee is most pleased.

Erasmus (the glory of *Netherland*, and the refiner of the Latin Tongue) wrote a whole Booke, in *the prayse of Folly*. Then if so excellent a Scholler, writ in praise of Vanity, why may not I write in praise of that which is profitable? There are no two Countreys, where Gold is esteemed, lesse than in *India*, and more then in *England*: the reason is, because the *Indians* are barbarous, and our Nation ciuill.

I have giuen *Pecunia* the title of a Woman, Both for the termination of the Word, and because (as Women are) shee is lov'd of men. The brauest Voyages in the World, haue beene made for Gold: for it, men haue venterd (by Sea) to the furthest parts of the Earth: In the Pursute whereof, *Englands Nestor* and *Neptune* (*Haukins* and *Drake*) lost their liues. Vpon the Deathes of the which two, of the first I writ this:

The Waters were his Winding sheete, the Sea was made his Toome;
Yet for his fame the Ocean Sea, was not sufficient roome.

Of the latter this:

England *his hart; his Corps the Waters haue;*
And that which raysd his fame, became his grave.

The *Prætorians* (after the death of *Pertinax*) in the election of a new Emperour, more esteemed the money of *Iulianus*, then either the vertue of *Seuerus*, or the Valour of *Pessennius*. Then of what great estimation and account, this Lady *Pecunia*, both hath beene in the Worlde, and is at this present, I leaue to your Iudgement. But what speake I so much of her praise in my Epistle, that haue commended her so at large in my Booke? To the reading wherof, (Gentlemen) I referre you.

[THE AUTHORS FIRST EPISTLE-DEDICATORY (1605).

[Collated with the Bridgwater House copy.]

Ed by the swift report of winged Fame,
   With siluer trumpet, sounding forth your name
   To you I dedicate this merry Muse,
And for my Patron, I your fauour chuse:
  She is a Lady, she must be respected:
She is a Queene, she may not be neglected.
  This is the shadow, you the substance haue,
   Which substance now this shadow seems to craue.

RICHARD BARNFIELD.]

The prayse of Lady Pecunia.

Sing not of *Angellica* the faire,
(For whom the Palladine of *Fraunce* fell mad)
Nor of sweet *Rosamond*, olde *Cliffords* heire,
(Whose death did make the second *Henry* sad)
  But of the fairest Faire *Pecunia*,
  The famous Queene of rich *America*.

Goddesse of Golde, great Empresse of the Earth,
O thou that canst doe all Thinges vnder Heauen:
That doost conuert the saddest minde to Mirth;
(Of whom the elder Age was quite bereauen)
  Of thee Ile sing, and in thy Prayse Ile write;
  You *golden Angels* helpe me to indite.

You, you alone, can make my Muse to speake;
And tell a golden Tale, with siluer Tongue:
You onely can my pleasing silence breake;
And adde some Musique, to a merry Songue:
  But amongst all the fiue, in Musicks Art,
  I would not sing the *Counter*-tenor part.

The Meane is best, and that I meane to keepe;
So shall I keepe my selfe from That I meane:
Lest with some Others, I be forc'd to weepe,
And cry *Peccaui*, in a dolefull Scæne.
  But to the matter which I haue in hand,
  The Lady Regent, both by Sea and Land.

When *Saturne* liu'd, and wore the Kingly Crowne,
(And *Ioue* was yet vnborne, but not vnbred)
This Ladies fame was then of no renowne ;
(For Golde was then, no more esteem'd then Lead)
   Then Truth and Honesty were onely vs'd,
   Siluer and Golde were vtterly refus'd.

But when the Worlde grew wiser in Conceit,
And saw how Men in manners did decline,
How Charitie began to loose her heate,
And One did at anothers good repine,
   Then did the Aged, first of all respect her ;
   And vowd from thenceforth, neuer to reiect her.

Thus with the Worlde, her beauty did increase ;
And manie Suters had she to obtaine her :
Some sought her in the Wars, and some in peace ;
But few of youthfull age, could euer gaine her :
   Or if they did, she soone was gone againe ;
   And would with them, but little while remaine.

For why against the Nature of her Sexe,
(That commonlie dispise the feeble Olde)
Shee, loues olde men ; but young men she reiects ;
Because to her, their Loue is quicklie colde :
   Olde men (like Husbands iealous of their Wiues)
   Lock her vp fast, and keepe her as their Liues.

The young man carelesse to maintaine his life,
Neglects her Loue (as though he did abhor her)
Like one that hardly doeth obtaine a wife,
And when he hath her once, he cares not for her :
   Shee, seeing that the young man doeth despyse her,
   Leaues the franke heart, and flies vnto the Myser.

Hee intertaines her, with a ioyfull hart ;
And seemes to rue her vndeserued wrong :
And from his Pressence, she shall neuer part ;
Or if shee doo, he thinkes her Absence long :
   And oftentimes he sends for her againe,
   Whose life without her, cannot long remaine.

And when he hath her, in his owne possession,
He locks her in an iron-barred Chest,
And doubting somewhat, of the like Transgression,
He holds that iron-walled Prison best.
  And least some *rusty* sicknesse should infect her,
  He often visits her, and doeth respect her.

As for the young man (subiect vnto sinne)
No maruell though the Diuell doe distresse him;
To tempt mans frailtie, which doth neuer linne,
Who many times, hath not a *Crosse* to blesse him:
  But how can hee incurre the Heauens Curse,
  That hath so many *Crosses* in his Purse?

Hee needes not feare those wicked sprights, that waulke
Vnder the Couerture of cole-blacke Night;
For why the Diuell still, a *Crosse* doeth baulke,
Because on it, was hangd the Lorde of Light:
  But let not Mysers trust to *siluer Crosses*,
  Least in the End, their gaines be turnd to losses.

But what care they, so they may hoorde vp golde?
Either for God, or Diuell, or Heauen, or Hell?
So they may faire *Pecuniaes* face behold;
And euery Day, their Mounts of Money tell.
  What tho to count their Coyne, they neuer blin,
  Count they their Coyne, and counts not God their sin?

But what talke I of sinne, to Vsurers?
Or looke for mendment, at a Mysers hand?
Pecunia, hath so many followers,
Bootlesse it is, her Power to with-stand.
  King *Couetise*, and *Warinesse* his Wife,
  The Parents were, that first did giue her Life.

But now vnto her Praise I will proceede,
Which is as ample, as the Worlde is wide:
What great Contentment doth her Pressence breede
In him, that can his wealth with Wysdome guide?
  She is the Soueraigne Queene, of all Delights:
  For her the Lawyer pleades; the Souldier fights.

For her, the Merchant venters on the Seas:
For her, the Scholler studdies at his Booke:
For her, the Vsurer (with greater ease)
For sillie fishes, layes a siluer hooke:
   For her, the Townsman leaues the Countrey Village:
   For her, the Plowman giues himselfe to Tillage.

For her, the Gentlemen doeth raise his rents:
For her, the Seruingman attends his maister:
For her, the curious head new toyes inuents:
For her, to Sores, the Surgeon layes his plaister.
   In fine for her, each man in his Vocation,
   Applies himselfe, in euerie sev'rall Nation.

What can thy hart desire, but thou mayst haue it,
If thou hast readie money to disburse?
Then thanke thy Fortune, that so freely gaue it;
For of all friends, the surest is thy purse.
   Friends may proue false, and leaue thee in thy need;
   But still thy Purse will bee thy friend indeed.

Admit thou come, into a place vnknowne;
And no man knowes, of whence, or what thou art:
If once thy faire *Pecunia*, shee be showne,
Thou art esteem'd a man of great Desart:
   And placed at the Tables vpper ende;
   Not for thine owne sake, but thy faithfull frende.

But if you want your Ladies louely grace,
And haue not wherewithall to pay your shot,
Your Hostis pressently will step in Place,
You are a Stranger (Sir) I know you not:
   By trusting Diuers, I am run in Det;
   Therefore of mee, nor meate nor Bed you get.

O who can then, expresse the worthie praise,
Which faire *Pecunia* iustly doeth desarue?
That can the meanest man, to Honor raise;
And feed the soule, that ready is to starue.
   Affection, which was wont to bee so pure,
   Against a golden Siege, may not endure.

Witnesse the trade of Mercenary sinne;
(Or Occupation, if thou list to tearme it)
Where faire *Pecunia* must the suite beginne;
(As common-tride Experience doeth confirme it)
   Not *Mercury* himselfe, with siluer Tongue,
   Can so inchaunt, as can a golden Songue.

When nothing could subdue the *Phrygian Troy*,
(That Citty through the world so much renowned)
Pecunia did her vtterly destroy:
And left her fame, in darke Obliuion drowned.
   And many Citties since, no lesse in fame,
   For Loue of her, haue yeelded to their shame.

What Thing is then, so well belou'd as money?
It is a speciall Comfort to the minde;
More faire then Women are; more sweet then honey:
Easie to loose, but very harde to finde.
   In fine, to him, whose Purse beginns to faint,
   Golde is a God, and Siluer is a Saint.

The Tyme was once, when Honestie was counted
A Demy god; and so esteem'd of all:
But now *Pecunia* on his Seate is mounted;
Since Honestie in great Disgrace did fall.
   No state, no Calling now, doeth him esteeme;
   Nor of the other ill, doeth any deeme.

The reason is, because he is so poore:
(And who respects the poore, and needie Creature?)
Still begging of his almes, from Doore to Doore:
All ragd, and torne; and eeke deformed in feature.
   In Countinance so changde, that none can know him;
   So weake, and euery vice doeth ouerthrow him.

But faire *Pecunia*, (most diuinely bred)
For sundrie shapes, doth *Proteus* selfe surpasse:
In one Lande, she is suted all in Lead;
And in another, she is clad in Brasse:
   But still within the Coast of *Albion*,
   She euer puts, her best Apparell on.

Siluer and Golde, and nothing else is currant,
In *Englands*, in faire *Englands* happy Land:
All baser sorts of Mettalls, haue no Warrant;
Yet secretly they *slip*, from hand to hand.
  If any such be tooke, the same is lost,
  And pressently is nayled on a Post.

Which with Quick-siluer, being flourisht ouer,
Seemes to be perfect Siluer, to the showe:
As Woemens paintings, their defects doe couer,
Vnder this false attyre, so doe they goe.
  If on a woollen Cloth, thou rub the same,
  Then will it straight beginne to blush, for shame.

If chafed on thy haire, till it be hot,
If it good Siluer bee, the scent is sweete:
If counterfeit, thy chafing hath begot
A ranke-smelt sauour; for a Queene vnmeete:
  Pecunia is a Queene, for her Desarts,
  And in the Decke, may goe for *Queene of harts*.

The Queene of harts, because she rules all harts;
And hath all harts, obedient to her Will:
Whose Bounty, fame vnto the Worlde imparts;
And with her glory, all the Worlde doeth fill:
  The *Queene of Diamonds*, she cannot bee;
  There is but one, E L I Z A , thou art shee.

And thou art shee, O sacred Soueraigne;
Whom God hath helpt with his Al-mighty hand:
Blessing thy People, with thy peacefull raigne;
And made this little Land, a happy Land:
  May all those liue, that wish long life to thee,
  And all the rest, perish eternally.

Thy tyme was once, when faire *Pecunia*, here
Did basely goe attyred all in Leather:
But since her raigne, she neuer did appeere
But richly clad; in Golde, or Siluer either:
  Nor reason is it, that her Golden raigne
  With baser Coyne, eclypsed should remaine.

And as the Coyne, she hath repurifyde,
From baser substance, to the purest Mettels:
Religion so, hath shee refinde beside,
From Papistrie, to Truth; which daily settles
   Within her Peoples harts; though some there bee,
   That cleaue vnto their wonted Papistrie.

No flocke of sheepe, but some are still infected:
No peece of Lawne so pure, but hath some fret:
All buildings are not strong, that are erected:
All Plants proue not, that in good ground are set:
   Some tares are sowne, amongst the choicest seed:
   No garden can be cleansd of euery Weede.

But now to her, whose praise is her pretended,
(Diuine *Pecunia*) fairer then the morne:
Which cannot be sufficiently commended;
Whose Sun-bright Beauty doeth the Worlde adorne,
   Adorns the World, but specially the Purse;
   Without whose pressence, nothing can be worse.

Not faire *Hæsione* (King of *Priams* sister)
Did euer showe more Beauty, in her face,
Then can this louely Lady, if it list her
To showe her selfe; admir'd for comely grace:
   Which neither Age can weare, nor Tyme conclude;
   For why, her Beauty yeerely is renude.

New Coyne is coynd each yeare, within the Tower;
So that her Beauty neuer can decay:
Which to resist, no mortall man hath Power,
When as she doeth her glorious Beames display.
   Nor doeth *Pecunia*, onely please the eie,
   But charms the eare, with heauenly Harmonie.

Lyke to an other *Orpheus*, can she play
Vpon her *treble Harpe*, whose siluer sound
Inchaunts the eare, and steales the hart away:
Nor hardly can deceit, therein be found.
   Although such Musique, some a Shilling cost,
   Yet is it worth but *Nine-pence*, at the most.

Had I the sweet inchaunting Tongue of *Tully*,
That charmd the hearers, lyke the Syrens Song ;
Yet could I not describe the Prayses fully,
Which to *Pecunia* iustly doe belong.
   Let it suffice, her Beauty doeth excell :
   Whose praise no Pen can paint, no Tongue can tell.

Then how shall I describe, with artlesse Pen,
The praise of her, whose praise, all praise surmounteth ?
Breeding amazement, in the mindes of men :
Of whom, this pressent Age to much accounteth.
   Varietie of Words, would sooner want,
   Then store of plentious matter, would be scant.

Whether yee list, to looke into the Citty :
(Where money tempts the poore Beholders eye)
Or to the Countrey Townes, devoyde of Pitty :
(Where to the poore, each place doeth almes denye)
   All Thinges for money now, are bought and solde,
   That either hart can thinke, or eie beholde.

Nay more for money (as report doeth tell)
Thou mayst obteine a Pardon for thy sinnes :
The Pope of *Rome*, for money will it sell ;
(Whereby thy soule, no small saluation winnes)
   But how can hee, (of Pride the chiefe Beginner)
   Forgiue thy sinnes, that is himselfe a sinner ?

Then, sith the Pope is subiect vnto sinne,
No maruell tho, diuine *Pecunia* tempt him,
With her faire Beauty ; whose good-will to winne,
Each one contends ; and shall we then exempt him.
   Did neuer mortall man, yet looke vpon her,
   But straightwaies he became, enamourd on her.

Yet would I wish, the Wight that loues her so,
And hath obtain'd, the like good-will againe,
To vse her wisely, lest she proue his foe ;
And so, in stead of Pleasure, breed his paine.
   She may be kyst ; but shee must not be *clypt* :
   Lest such Delight in bitter gall be dypt.

The iuyce of grapes, which is a soueraigne Thing
To cheere the hart, and to reuiue the spirits ;
Being vsde immoderatly (in surfetting)
Rather Dispraise, then commendation merits:
  Euen so *Pecunia*, is, as shee is vsed ;
  Good of her selfe, but bad if once abused.

With her, the Tenant payes his Landlords rent :
On her, depends the stay of euery state :
To her, rich Pressents euery day are sent :
In her, it rests to end all dire Debate :
  Through her, to Wealth, is raisd the Countrey Boore :
  From her, proceedes much proffit to the poore.

Then how can I, sufficiently commend,
Her Beauties worth, which makes the World to wonder?
Or end her prayse, whose prayses haue no End?
Whose absence brings the stoutest stomack vnder :
  Let it suffice, *Pecunia* hath no peere ;
  No Wight, no Beauty held ; more faire, more deere.

FINIS.

His Prayer to Pecunia.

Reat Lady, sith I haue complyde thy Prayse,
(According to my skill and not thy merit :)
And sought thy Fame aboue the starrs to rayse ;
(Had I sweete *Ovids* vaine, or *Virgils* spirit)
  I craue no more but this, for my good will,
  That in my Want, thou wilt supplye me still.

THE
Complaint of Poetrie,
for the Death of Liberalitie.

Viuit post funera virtus.

LONDON,
Printed by G. S. for Iohn Iaggard, and are
to be solde at his shoppe neere Temple-barre,
at the Signe of the Hand and starre.
1598.

THE
Complaint of Poesie,
for the death of Liberalitie

To his Worshipfull wel-willer, Maister
Edward Leigh, of Grayes Inne.

IMage of that, whose losse is here lamented;
(In whom, so many vertues are containd)
Daine to accept, what I haue novv presented.
Though Bounties death, herein be not fained,
In your mind, she not reuiue (with speed)
Then will I sweare, that shee is dead indeed.

THE COMPLAINT OF
Poetrie, for the Death of Liberalitie.

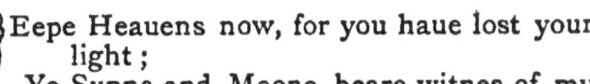Eepe Heauens now, for you haue lost your
light;
Ye Sunne and Moone, beare witnes of my
mone:
The cleere is turnd to clouds; the day to
night;
And all my hope, and all my ioy is gone:
   Bounty is dead, the cause of my annoy;
   Bounty is dead, and with her dide my ioy.

O who can comfort my afflicted soule?
Or adde some ende to my increasing sorrowes?
Who can deliuer me from endlesse dole?
(Which from my hart eternall torment borrowes.)
   When *Bounty* liu'd, I bore the Bell away;
   When *Bounty* dide, my credit did decay.

I neuer then, did write one verse in vaine;
Nor euer went my Poems vnregarded:
Then did each Noble breast, me intertaine,
And for my Labours I was well rewarded:
   But now *Good wordes*, are stept in *Bounties* place,
   Thinking thereby, her glorie to disgrace.

The Complaint of Poetrie.

But who can liue with words, in these hard tymes?
(Although they came from *Iupiter* himselfe?)
Or who can take such Paiment, for his Rymes?
(When nothing now, is so esteem'd as Pelfe?)
   Tis not *Good wordes*, that can a man maintaine;
   Wordes are but winde; and winde is all but vaine.

Where is *Mecænas*, Learnings noble Patron?
(That *Maroes* Muse, with Bountie so did cherish?)
Or faire *Zenobia*, that worthy Matron?
(Whose name, for Learnings Loue, shall neuer perish)
   What tho their Bodies, lie full lowe in graue,
   Their fame the worlde; their souls the Heauens haue.

Vile *Auaricia*, how hast thou inchaunted
The Noble mindes, of great and mightie Men?
Or what infernall furie late hath haunted
Their niggard purses? (to the learned pen)
   Was it *Augustus* wealth, or noble minde,
   That euerlasting fame, to him assinde?

If wealth? Why *Cræsus* was more rich then hee;
(Yet *Cræsus* glorie, with his life did end)
It was his Noble mind, that moued mee
To write his praise, and eeke his Acts commend.
   Who ere had heard, of *Alexanders* fame,
   If *Quintus Curtius* had not pend the same?

Then sith by mee, their deedes haue been declared,
(Which else had perisht with their liues decay)
Who to augment their glories, haue not spared
To crowne their browes, with neuer-fading Bay:
   What Art deserues such Liberalitie,
   As doeth the peerlesse Art of Poetrie?

But *Liberalitie* is dead and gone:
And *Auarice* vsurps true *Bounties* seat.
For her it is, I make this endlesse mone,
(Whose praises worth no men can well repeat.
   Sweet *Liberalitie* adiew for euer,
   For *Poetrie* againe, shall see thee neuer.

Neuer againe, shall I thy presence see:
Neuer againe, shal I thy bountie tast:
Neuer againe, shal I accepted bee:
Neuer againe, shall I be so embrac't:
  Neuer againe, shall I the bad recall:
  Neuer againe, shall I be lou'd of all:

Thou wast the Nurse, whose Bountie gaue me sucke:
Thou wast the Sunne, whose beames did lend me light:
Thou wast the Tree, whose fruit I still did plucke:
Thou wast the Patron, to maintaine my right:
  Through thee I liu'd; on thee I did relie;
  In thee I ioy'd; and now for thee I die.

What man, hath lately lost a faithfull frend?
Or Husband, is depriued of his Wife?
But doth his after-daies in dolour spend?
(Leading a loathsome, discontented life?)
  Dearer then friend, or wife, haue I forgone;
  Then maruell not, although I make such mone.

Faire *Philomela*, cease thy sad complaint;
And lend thine eares, vnto my dolefull Ditty:
(Whose soule with sorrowe, now begins to faint,
And yet I cannot moue mens hearts to pitty:)
  Thy woes are light, compared vnto mine:
  You waterie Nymphes, to mee your plaints resigne.

And thou *Melpomene*, (the Muse of Death)
That neuer sing'st, but in a dolefull straine;
Sith cruell Destinie hath stopt her breath,
(Who whilst she liu'd, was Vertues Soueraigne
  Leaue *Hellicon*, (whose bankes so pleasant bee)
  And beare a part of sorrowe now with mee.

The Trees (for sorrowe) shead their fading Leaues,
And weepe out gum, in stead of other teares;
Comfort nor ioy, no Creature now conceiues,
To chirpe and sing, each little bird forbeares.
  The sillie Sheepe, hangs downe his drooping head,
  And all because, that *Bounty* she is dead.

The greater that I feele my griefe to be,
The lesser able, am I to expresse it;
Such is the nature of extremitie,
The heart it som-thing eases, to confesse it.
   Therefore Ile wake my muse, amidst her sleeping,
   And what I want in wordes, supplie with weeping.

Weepe still mine eies, a Riuer full of Teares,
To drowne my Sorrowe in, that so molests me;
And rid my head of cares; my thoughts of feares:
Exiling sweet Content, that so detests me.
   But ah (alas) my Teares are almost dun,
   And yet my griefe, it is but new begun.

Euen as the Sunne, when as it leaues our sight,
Doth shine with those Antipodes, beneath vs;
Lending the other worlde her glorious light,
And dismall Darknesse, onely doeth bequeath vs:
   Euen so sweet *Bountie*, seeming dead to mee,
   Liues now to none, but smooth-Tongd Flatterie.

O *Adulation*, Canker-worme of Truth;
The flattring Glasse of Pride, and Self-conceit:
(Making olde wrinkled Age, appeare like youth)
Dissimulations Maske, and follies Beate:
   Pittie it is, that thou art so rewarded,
   Whilst Truth and Honestie, goe vnregarded.

O that Nobilitie, it selfe should staine,
In being bountifull, to such vile Creatures:
Who, when they flatter most, then most they faine;
Knowing what humor best, will fit their Natures.
   What man so mad, that knowes himselfe but pore,
   And will beleeue that he hath riches store.

Vpon a time, the craftie Foxe did flatter
The foolish Pye (whose mouth was full of meate)
The Pye beleeuing him, began to chatter,
And sing for ioy, (not hauing list to eate)
   And whil'st the foolish Pye, her meate let fall,
   The craftie Foxe, did runne awaie with all.

Terence describeth vnder *Gnatoes* name,
The right conditions of a Parasyte:
(And with such Eloquence, sets foorth the same,
As doeth the learned Reader much delyght)
   Shewing, that such a Sycophant as *Gnato*,
   In more esteem'd, then twentie such a *Plato*.

Bounty looke backe, vpon thy goods mispent;
And thinke how ill, thou hast bestow'd thy mony:
Consider not their wordes, but their intent;
Their hearts are gall, although their tongues be hony:
   They speake not as they thinke, but all is fained,
   And onely to th'intent to be maintained.

And herein happie, I areade the poore;
No flattring Spanyels, fawne on them for meate:
The reason is, because the Countrey Boore
Hath little enough, for himselfe to eate:
   No man will flatter him, except himselfe;
   And why? because hee hath no store of wealth.

But sure it is not *Liberalitie*
That doeth reward these fawning smel-feasts so:
It is the vice of Prodigalitie,
That doeth the Bankers of *Bounty* over-flo:
   Bounty is dead: yea so it needes must bee;
   Or if aliue, yet is shee dead to mee.

Therefore as one, whose friend is lately dead,
I will bewaile the death, of my deere frend;
Vppon whose Tombe, ten thousand Teares Ile shead,
Till drearie Death, of mee shall make an end:
   Or if she want a Toombe, to her desart,
   Oh then, Ile burie her within my hart.

But (*Bounty*) if thou loue a Tombe of stone,
Oh then seeke out, a hard and stonie hart:
For were mine so, yet would it melt with mone,
And all because, that I with thee must part.
   Then, if a stonie hart must thee interr,
   Goe finde a Step-dame, or a Vsurer.

And sith there dies no Wight, of great account,
But hath an Epitaph compos'd by mee,
Bounty, that did all other far surmount,
Vpon her Tombe, this Epitaph shall bee:
  Here lies the Wight, that Learning did maintaine,
  And at the last, by A V A R I C E *was slaine.*

Vile *Auarice*, why hast thou kildd my Deare?
And robd the World, of such a worthy Treasure?
In whome no sparke of goodnesse doth appeare,
So greedie is thy mind, without all measure,
  Thy death, from Death did merit to release her:
  The Murtherers deseru'd to die, not *Caesar*.

The Merchants wife; the Tender-hearted Mother
That leaues her loue; whose Sonne is prest for warre;
(Resting, the one; as woefull as fhe other;)
Hopes met at length, when ended is the iarre,
  To see her Husband; see her Sonne again;
  "Were it not then for Hope, the hart were slaine."

But I, whose hope is turned to despaire
Nere looke to see my dearest Deare againe:
Then *Pleasure* sit thou downe, in *Sorrowes* Chaire,
And (for a while) thy wonted Mirth refraine.
  Bounty is dead, that whylome was my Treasure,
  Bounty is dead, my joy and onely pleasure.

If *Pythias* death, of *Damon* were bewailed;
Or *Pillades* did rue, *Orestes* ende:
If *Hercules*, for *Hylas* losse were quailed;
Or *Theseus*, for *Pyrithous* Teares did spende:
  When doe I mourne for *Bounty*, being dead:
  Who liuing, was my hand, my hart, my head.

My hand, to helpe mee, in my greatest need:
My hart, to comfort mee, in my distresse:
My head, whom onely I obeyd, indeed:
If she were such, how can my griefe be lesse?
  Perhaps my wordes, may pierce the *Parcæ*'s eares;
  If not with wordes, Ile moue them with my teares.

But ah (alas) my Teares are spent in vaine,
(For she is dead, and I am left aliue)
Teares cannot call, sweet *Bounty* backe againe ;
Then why doe I, gainst Fate and Fortune striue ?
    And for her death, thus weepe, lament, and crie ;
    Sith euery mortall wight, is borne to die.

But as the woefull mother doeth lament,
Her tender babe, with cruell Death opprest :
Whose life was spotlesse, pure, and innocent,
(And therefore sure, it[s] soule is gone to rest)
    So *Bountie*, which her selfe did vpright keepe,
    Yet for her losse, loue cannot chuse but weepe.

The losse of her, is losse to many a one :
The losse of her, is losse vnto the poore :
And therefore not a losse, to mee alone,
But vnto such, as goe from Doore to Doore.
    Her losse, is losse vnto the fatherlesse ;
    And vnto all, that are in great distresse.

The maimed Souldier, comming from the warre,
The woefull wight, whose house was lately burnd ;
The sillie soule ; the wofull Traueylar ;
And all, whom Fortune at her feet hath spurnd ;
    Lament the losse of *Liberálitie* :
    "Its ease, to haue in griefe some Companie."

The Wife of *Hector* (sad *Andromache*)
Did not bewaile, her husbands death alone :
But (sith he was the *Troians* onely stay)
The wiues of *Troy* (for him) made æquall mone.
    Shee, shead the teares of Loue ; and they of pittie :
    Shee, for her deare dead Lord ; they, for their Cittie.

Nor is the Death of *Liberalitie*,
(Although my griefe be greater than the rest)
Onely lamented, and bewaild of mee ;
(And yet of mee, she was beloued best)
    But, sith she was so bountifull to all,
    She is lamented, both of great and small.

O that my Teares could moue the powres diuine,
That *Bountie* might be called from the dead :
As Pitty pierc'd the hart of *Proserpine*;
Who (moued with the Teares *Admetus* shead)
   Did sende him backe againe, his louing Wife ;
   Who lost her owne, to saue her husbands life.

Impartiall *Parcæ*, will no prayers moue you ?
Can Creatures so diuine, haue stony harts?
Haplesse are they, whose hap it is to proue you,
For you respect no Creatures good Desarts.
   O *Atropos*, (the cruelst of the three)
   Why hast thou tane, my faithfull friend from mee ?

But ah, she cannot (or shee will not) heare me,
Or if shee doo, yet may not she repent her :
Then come (sweet Death) O why doest thou forbeare me ?
Aye mee ! thy Dart is blunt, it will not enter.
   Oh now I knowe the cause, and reason why ;
   I am immortall, and I cannot dye.

So *Cytheræa* would haue dide, but could not ;
When faire *Adonis* by her side lay slaine :
So I desire the Sisters, what I should not ;
For why (alas) I wish for Death in vaine ;
   Death is their seruant, and obeys their will ;
   And if they bid him spare, he cannot kill.

Oh would I were, as other Creatures are ;
Then would I die, and so my griefe were ended :
But Death (against my will) my life doeth spare ;
(So little with the fates I am befrended)
   Sith, when I would, thou doost my sute denie,
   Vile Tyrant, when thou wilt, I will not die.

And *Bounty*, though her body thou hast slaine,
Yet shall her memorie remaine for euer :
For euer, shall her memorie remaine ;
Whereof no spitefull Fortune can bereaue her.
   Then Sorrowe cease, and wipe thy weeping eye ;
   For Fame shall liue, when all the World shall dye.

FINIS.

THE Combat, betweene Conscience and Couetousnesse,

in the minde of Man.

*quid non mortalia pectora cogis
Auri sacra fames?* Virgil.

LONDON,
Printed by G. S. for Iohn Iaggard, and are
to be solde at his shoppe neere Temple-barre,
at the Signe of the Hand and starre.
1598.

To his Worshipfull good friend,

Maister *Iohn Steuenton*, of *Dothill*, in the County of *Salop*, Esquire.

Ith Conscience (long since) is exilde the Citty,
   O let her in the Countrey, finde some Pitty:
But if she be exilde, the Countrey too,
   O let her finde, some fauour yet of you.

The Combat betweene Conscience
and Couetousnesse in the
mind of Man.

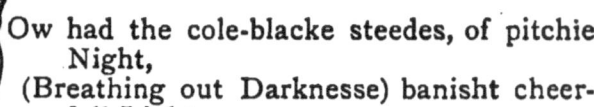Ow had the cole-blacke steedes, of pitchie
Night,
(Breathing out Darknesse) banisht cheer-
full Light,
And sleepe (the shaddowe of eternall rest)
My seuerall senses, wholy had possest.
When loe, there was presented to my view,
A vision strange, yet not so strange, as true.
Conscience (me thought) appeared vnto mee,
Cloth'd with good Deedes, with Trueth and Honestie,
Her countinance demure, and sober sad,
Nor any other Ornament shee had.
Then *Couetousnesse* did incounter her,
Clad in a Cassock, lyke a Vsurer,
The Cassock, it was made of poore-mens skinnes,
Lac'd here and there, with many seuerall sinnes:
Nor was it furd, with any common furre;
Or if it were, himselfe hee was the *fur*.
A Bag of money, in his hande he helde,
The which with hungry eie, he still behelde.
The place wherein this vision first began,
(A spacious plaine) was cald *The Minde of Man.*
The Carle no sooner, *Conscience* had espyde,
But swelling lyke a Toade, (puft vp with pryde)

He straight began against her to inuey:
These were the wordes, which *Couetise* did sey.
Conscience (quoth hee) how dar'st thou bee so bold,
To claime the place, that I by right doe hold?
Neither by right, nor might, thou canst obtaine it:
By might (thou knowst full well) thou canst not gaine it
The greatest Princes are my followars,
The King in Peace, the Captaine in the Warres:
The Courtier, and the simple Countrey-man:
The Iudge, the Merchant, and the Gentleman:
The learned Lawyer, and the Politician:
The skilfull Surgeon, and the fine Physician:
In briefe, all sortes of men mee entertaine,
And hold mee, as their Soules sole Soueraigne,
And in my quarrell, they will fight and die,
Rather then I should suffer iniurie.
And as for title, interest, and right,
Ile proue its mine by that, as well as might,
Though *Couetousnesse*, were vsed long before,
Yet *Iudas* Treason, made my Fame the more;
When *Christ* he caused, crucifyde to bee,
For thirtie pence, man solde his minde to mee:
And now adaies, what tenure is more free,
Than that which purchas'd is, with Gold and fee?

Conscience.

With patience, haue I heard thy large Complaint,
Wherein the Diuell, would be thought a Saint:
But wot ye what, the Saying is of olde?
One tale is good, vntill anothers tolde.
Truth is the right, that I must stand vpon,
(For other title, hath poore *Conscience* none)
First I will proue it, by Antiquitie,
That thou art but an vp-start, vnto mee;
Before that thou wast euer thought vpon,
The minde of Man, belongd to mee alone.
For after that the Lord, hath Man created,
And him in blisse-full Paradice had seated;
(Knowing his Nature was to vice inclynde)
God gaue me vnto man, to rule his mynde,
And as it were, his Gouernour to bee,

To guide his minde, in Trueth, and Honestie.
And where thou sayst, that man did sell his soule;
That Argument, I quicklie can controule:
It is a fayned fable, thou doost tell,
That, which is not his owne, he cannot sell;
No man can sell his soule, altho he thought it:
Mans soule is *Christs*, for hee hath dearely bought it.
Therefore vsurping *Couetise*, be gone.
For why, the minde belongs to mee alone.

Couetousnesse.

Alas poore *Conscience*, how thou art deceav'd?
As though of senses, thou wert quite bereaud.
What wilt thou say (that thinkst thou canst not erre)
If I can proue my selfe the ancienter?
Though into *Adams* minde, God did infuse thee,
Before his fall, yet man did neuer vse thee.
What was it else, but *Aurice* in *Eue*,
(Thinking thereby, in greater Blisse to liue)
That made her taste, of the forbidden fruite?
Of her Desier, was not I the roote?
Did she not couet? (tempted by the Deuill)
The Apple of the Tree, of good and euill?
Before man vsed *Conscience*, she did couet:
Therefore by her Transgression, here I proue it,
That *Couetousnesse* possest the minde of man,
Before that any *Conscience* began.

Conscience.

Euen as a counterfeited precious stone,
Seemes to bee far more rich, to looke vpon,
Then doeth the right: But when a man comes neere,
His basenes then, doeth euident appeere:
So *Couetise*, the Reasons thou doost tell,
Seeme to be strong, but being weighed well,
They are indeed, but onely meere Illusions,
And doe inforce but very weake Conclusions.
When as the Lord (fore-knowing his offence)
Had giuen man a Charge, of Abstinence,
And to refraine, the fruite of good and ill:
Man had a *Conscience*, to obey his will,

And neuer would be tempted thereunto,
Vntill the Woeman, shee, did worke *man woe*.
And make him breake, the Lords Commaundement,
Which all Mankinde, did afterward repent :
So that thou seest, thy Argument is vaine,
And I am prov'd, the elder of the twaine.

Couetousnesse.

Fond Wretch, it was not *Conscience*, but feare,
That made the first man (Adam) to forbeare
To tast the fruite, of the forbidden Tree,
Lest, if offending hee were found to bee,
(According as *Iehouah* saide on hye,
For his so great Transgression, hee should dye.)
Feare curbd his minde, it was not *Conscience* then,
(For *Conscience* freely, rules the harts of men)
And is a godly motion of the mynde,
To euerie vertuous action inclynde,
And not enforc'd, through feare of Punishment,
But is to vertue, voluntary bent :
Then (simple Trul) be packing presentlie,
For in this place, there is no roome for thee.

Conscience.

Aye mee (distressed Wight) what shall I doe?
Where shall I rest ? Or whither shall I goe ?
Vnto the rich ? (woes mee) they, doe abhor me :
Vnto the poore? (alas) they, care not for me :
Vnto the Olde-man ? hee ; hath mee forgot :
Vnto the Young-man ? yet hee, knowes me not :
Vnto the Prince ? hee ; can dispence with me :
Vnto the Magistrate ? that, may not bee :
Vnto the Court ? for it, I am too base :
Vnto the Countrey? there, I haue no place :
Vnto the Citty ? thence ; I am exilde :
Vnto the Village? there ; I am reuilde :
Vnto the Barre? the Lawyer there, is bribed ?
Vnto the Warre ? there, *Conscience* is derided :
Vnto the Temple ? there, I am disguised :
Vnto the Market ? there, I am dispised :
Thus both the young and olde, the rich and poore,

Against mee (silly Creature) shut their doore.
Then, sith each one seekes my rebuke and shame,
Ile goe againe to Heauen (from whence I came.)
   This saide (me thought) making exceeding mone,
She went her way, and left the Carle alone,
Who vaunting of his late-got victorie,
Aduanc'd himselfe in pompe and Maiestie:
Much like a Cocke, who hauing kild his foe,
Brisks vp himselfe, and then begins to crow.
So *Couetise*, when *Conscience* was departed,
Gan to be proud in minde, and hauty harted:
And in a stately Chayre of state he set him,
(For *Conscience* banisht) there are none to let him.
And being but one entrie, to this Plaine,
(Whereof as king and Lord, he did remaine)
Repentance cald, he causd that to be kept,
Lest *Conscience* should returne, whilst as he slept:
Wherefore he causd it, to be watcht and warded
Both night and Day, and to be strongly guarded:
To keepe it safe, these three he did intreat,
Hardnesse of hart, with *Falshood* and *Deceat*:
And if at any time, she chaunc'd to venter,
Hardnesse of hart, denide her still to enter.
When *Conscience* was exilde the minde of Man,
Then *Couetise*, his gouernment began.
This once being seene, what I had seene before,
(Being onely seene in sleepe) was seene no more;
For with the sorrowe, which my Soule did take
At sight hereof, foorthwith I did awake.

FINIS.

Poems:

In diuers humors.

Trabit sua quemque voluptas. Virgil.

LONDON,
Printed by G. S. for Iohn Iaggard, and are
to be solde at his shoppe neere Temple-barre,
at the Signe of the Hand and starre.
1598.

To the learned, and accomplisht Gentleman,
Maister *Nicholas Blackleech*,
of Grayes Inne.

TO you, that know the tuch of true Conceat;
(Whose many gifts I neede not to repeat)
I vvrite these Lines; fruits of vnriper yeares;
Wherein my Muse no harder censure feares:
Hoping in gentle Worth, you will them take;
Not for the gift, but for the giuers sake.

SONNET. I.

To his friend Maister R. L.   In praise of Musique and Poetrie.

F Musique and sweet Poetrie agree,
   As they must needes (the Sister and the Brother)
  Then must the Loue be great, twixt thee and mee,
   Because thou lou'st the one, and I the other.
Dowland to thee is deare; whose heauenly tuch
Vpon the Lute, doeth rauish humaine sense:
Spenser to mee; whose deepe Conceit is such,
   As passing all Conceit, needs no defence.
  Thou lou'st to heare the sweete melodious sound,
That *Phœbus* Lute (the Queene of Musique) makes:
And I in deepe Delight am chiefly drownd,
   When as himselfe to singing he betakes.
    One God is God of Both (as Poets faigne)
    One Knight loues Both, and Both in thee remaine.

SONNET. II.

Against the Dispraysers of Poetrie.

Haucer is dead; and *Gower* lyes in grave;
  The Earle of *Surrey*, long agoe is gone;
  Sir *Philip Sidneis* soule, the Heauens haue;
  George Gascoigne him beforne, was tomb'd in stone,
    Yet, tho their Bodies lye full low in ground,
  (As euery thing must dye, that earst was borne)
  Their liuing fame, no Fortune can confound;
  Nor euer shall their Labours be forlorne.
    And you, that discommend sweete Poetrie,
  (So that the Subiect of the same be good)
  Here may you see, your fond simplicitie;
  Sith Kings haue fauord it, of royall Blood.
    The King of *Scots* (now liuing) is a Poet,
    As his *Lepanto*, and his *Furies* shoe it.

A Remembrance of some English Poets.

Iue *Spenser* euer, in thy *Fairy Queene*:
  Whose like (for deepe Conceit) was neuer seene.
  Crownd mayst thou bee, vnto thy more renowne,
  (As King of Poets) with a Lawrell Crowne.

And *Daniell*, praised for thy sweet-chast Verse:
Whose Fame is grav'd on *Rosamonds* blacke Herse.
Still mayst thou liue: and still be honored,
For that rare Worke, *The White Rose and the Red*.

And *Drayton*, whose wel-written Tragedies,
And sweete Epistles, soare thy fame to skies.
Thy learned Name, is æquall with the rest;
Whose stately Numbers are so well addrest.

And *Shakespeare* thou, whose hony-flowing Vaine,
(Pleasing the World) thy Praises doth obtaine.
Whose *Venus*, and whose *Lucrece* (sweete, and chaste)
Thy Name in fames immortall Booke haue plac't.
 Liue euer you, at least in Fame liue euer:
Well may the Bodye dye, but Fame dies neuer.

An Ode.

AS it fell vpon a Day,
 In the merrie Month of May,
 Sitting in a pleasant shade,
 Which a groue of Myrtles made,
 Beastes did leape, and Birds did sing,
 Trees did grow, and Plants did spring:
 Euery thing did banish mone,
 Saue the Nightingale alone.
 Shee (poore Bird) as all forlorne,
 Leand her Breast vp-till a Thorne,
 And there sung the dolefulst Ditty,
 That to heare it was great Pitty.
 Fie, fie, fie, now would she cry
 Teru Teru, by and by:
 That to heare her so complaine,
 Scarce I could from Teares refraine:
 For her griefes so liuely showne,
 Made me thinke vpon mine owne.
 Ah (thought I) thou mournst in vaine;
 None takes Pitty on thy paine:
 Senslesse Trees, they cannot heere thee;
 Ruthlesse Beares, they wil not cheer thee.
 King *Pandion*, hee is dead:
 All thy friends are lapt in Lead.
 All thy fellow Birds doe singe,
 Carelesse of thy sorrowing.

Whilst as fickle Fortune smilde,
Thou and I, were both beguilde.
Euerie one that flatters thee,
Is no friend in miserie:
Words are easie, like the winde;
Faithfull friends are hard to finde:
Euerie man will bee thy friend,
Whilst thou hast wherewith to spend:
But if store of Crownes be scant,
No man will supply thy want.
If that one be prodigall,
Bountifull, they will him call.
And with such-like flattering,
Pitty but hee were a King.
If hee bee adict to vice,
Quickly him, they will intice.
If to Woemen hee be bent,
They haue at Commaundement.
But if Fortune once doe frowne,
Then farewell his great renowne:
They that fawnd on him before,
Vse his company no more.
Hee that is thy friend indeed,
Hee will helpe thee in thy neede:
If thou sorrowe, hee will weepe:
If thou wake, hee cannot sleepe:
Thus of euerie griefe, in hart,
Hee, with thee, doeth beare a Part.
These are certaine Signes, to knowe
Faithfull friend, from flatt'ring foe.

Written, at the Request of a Gentleman,

vnder a Gentlewoman's Picture.

Uen as *Apelles* could not paint *Campaspes* face aright:
Because *Campaspes* Sun-bright eyes did dimme *Apelles* sight:
Euen so, amazed at her sight, her sight, all sights excelling,
Like *Nyobe* the Painter stoode, her sight his sight expelling,
Thus Art and Nature did contend, who should the Victor bee,
Till Art by Nature was supprest, as all the worlde may see.

An Epitaph vpon the Death, of Sir Philip

Sidney, Knight; Lord-gouernour of Vlissing.

Hat *England* lost, that Learning lov'd, that euery mouth commended,
That fame did prayse, that Prince did rayse, that Countrey do defended,
Here lyes the man: lyke to the Swan, who knowing shee shall die,
Doeth tune her voice vnto the Spheares, and scornes Mortalitie.
Two worthie Earls his vncles were; a Lady was his Mother;
A Knight his father; and himselfe a noble Countesse Brother.
Belov'd, bewaild; aliue, now dead; of all, with Teares for euer;
Here lyes Sir *Philip Sidneis* Corps, whom cruell Death did seuer,
He liv'd for her, hee dyde for her; for whom he dyde, he liued:
O graunt (O God) that wee of her, may neuer be depriued.

An Epitaph vpon the Death of his Aunt,
Mistresse Elizabeth Skrymsher.

LOe here beholde the certaine Ende, of euery liuing wight:
No Creature is secure from Death, for Death will haue his Right.
He spareth none: both rich and poore, both young and olde must die;
So fraile is flesh, so short is Life, so sure Mortalitie.
When first the Bodye liues to Life, the soule first dies to sinne:
And they that loose this earthly Life, a heauenly Life shall winne,
If they liue well: as well she liv'd, that lyeth Vnder heere;
Whose Vertuous Life to all the Worlde, most plainly did appeere.
Good to the poore, friend to the rich, and foe to no Degree:
A President of modest Life, and peerelesse Chastitie.
Who louing more, Who more belov'd of euerie honest mynde?
Who more to Hospitalitie, and Clemencie inclinde
Then she? that being buried here, lyes wrapt in Earth below;
From whence we came, to whom wee must, and bee as shee is now,
A Clodd of Clay: though her pure soule in endlesse Blisse doeth rest;
Ioying all Ioy, the Place of Peace, prepared for the blest:
Where holy Angells sit and sing, before the King of Kings;
Not mynding worldly Vanities, but onely heavenly Things.
Vnto which Ioy, Vnto which Blisse, Vnto which Place of Pleasure,
God graunt that wee may come at last, t' inioy that heauenly Treasure.
Which to obtaine, to liue as shee hath done let us endeuor;
That wee may liue with Christ himselfe, (above) that liues for euer.

A Comparison of the Life of Man.

Ans life is vvell compared to a feast,
Furnisht with choice of all Varietie :
To it comes Tyme ; and as a bidden guest
Hee sets him downe, in Pompe and Maiestie ;
The three-folde Age of Man, the Waiters bee,
   Then with an earthen voyder (made of clay)
   Comes Death, and takes the table clean
       away.

F I N I S.

www.ingramcontent.com/pod-product-compliance
Lightning Source LLC
Chambersburg PA
CBHW030355170426
43202CB00010B/1379